Harvard Studies in Urban History

Series Editors

Stephan Thernstrom
Charles Tilly

The Glassworkers of Carmaux

*French Craftsmen and Political Action
in a Nineteenth-Century City*

Joan Wallach Scott

*Harvard University Press
Cambridge, Massachusetts
London, England*

For my parents, Lottie and Samuel Wallach,
and to the memory of Rose V. Russell

Acknowledgments

Most of the research for this book was done in France at the Archives Nationales, the Bibliothèque Nationale, the Archives Departémentales du Tarn, and the Archives Municipales de Carmaux. The director and staff of the Archives du Tarn provided a great deal of assistance, for which I am most grateful. The staff at the Bureau d'état civil in the Hôtel de Ville at Carmaux not only furnished the records I needed but made a long, often dull task endurable and enjoyable. Their memories and anecdotes about their grandparents, the glassworkers and miners of Carmaux, gave me a sense of my subject that no archival sources could provide.

A University of Wisconsin Alumni Research Foundation Fellowship and a Research Training Fellowship from the Social Sciences Research Council provided needed financial assistance. The SSRC grant also provided important technical training in sociology and historical demography.

I wish to thank the following for granting me permission to use materials for which they hold the copyright:

Editions Ouvrières for permission to quote from Rolande Trempé's *Les Mineurs de Carmaux* (1971); Mouton and Co. for permission to reproduce a section of a table from André

Acknowledgments

Armengaud's *Les Populations de l'Est-Aquitain au début de l'époque contemporaine* (1961); Yale University Press for permission to incorporate parts of my article, "The Glassworkers of Carmaux," in S. Thernstrom and R. Sennett, eds., *Nineteenth Century Cities: Essays in the New Urban History* (1969); the editors of *Le Mouvement Social* for permission to incorporate parts of my article, "Les Verriers de Carmaux," no. 76 (1971); Bernard Moss for permission to quote from his unpublished dissertation, "Origins of the French Labor Movement: The Socialism of Skilled Workers," Columbia University, 1972; Monsieur Lucien Renoux, for permission to quote from his father's archives and to use copies of photographs in his collection.

All translations from these materials and from other sources cited in the text are my own.

A number of friends and colleagues read this manuscript at various stages. Their criticisms have improved it immeasurably. From them I learned what it meant to be a part of a community of scholars. I am thankful for the help of Richard Hellie, William Sewell, Jr., J. Harvey Smith, Stephan Thernstrom, and Charles Tilly. The comments of Herbert Gutman, whose sensitivity to and enthusiasm for this kind of social history are a model for my own work, were most helpful in the final stages of revising the manuscript.

Several friends and teachers have had a formative role in my development as a historian, as well as in the shaping of this book. First among them is my husband, Donald Moore Scott. He knows how grateful I am. Rolande Trempé of the University of Toulouse introduced me to local archival sources. She never hesitated to share the information she gained in her monumental work on the miners of Carmaux and she taught me a great deal. In every sense of her use of the term she was a true intellectual "comrade." The commitment of my dissertation director, Harvey Goldberg, inspired me to study the French working-class movement. It was he who originally suggested that I investigate Carmaux. I deeply appreciate his help. William R. Taylor first taught me to ask the questions I have learned to ask of historical materials. His example and his teaching were among the most important influences I experienced as a graduate student. I owe him a great intellectual debt. It was also in his seminar that I first read the two books which helped shape this study: E. P. Thompson's *The Making of the English Working Class* and Stephan Thernstrom's, *Poverty and Progress: Social Mobility in Newburyport.* By far the most critical influence in my own intellectual history has been Charles Tilly. Under his guidance I learned how to do social history. His training has developed my substantive and theoretical understanding as well as my critical judgment and discipline. I think of my relation to him as that of the apprentice to the master crafts-man and, like a young glassworker, it is to the master's tutelage that I ultimately owe my own skill. Like a young craftsman, too, I alone am responsible for any faults in my work.

Joan Wallach Scott

Chicago, Illinois
1972

Contents

Introduction   1

1 Carmaux, 1850–1890   7

2 The Craft of the Glassworker   19

3 Glassworkers and Miners: A Contrast   53

4 Mechanization   72

5 Socialism   108

6 The Strike of 1895   139

7 New Glassworkers and Old, 1896–1914   167

Epilogue: Three Portraits   193

Appendix   203

Bibliography   207

Notes   217

Index   237

Illustrations

Plates I–VII. The art of making glass bottles, France. 24
(From the *Encyclopédie, ou Dictionnaire raisonné des Sciences, des arts et des métiers. Recueil de planches sur les sciences, les arts libéraux et les arts méchaniques, avec leur explication. Vol. X [Paris, 1772].)*

1. Main entrance to the Verrerie Sainte Clothilde, 1895. 144

2. Jaurès leading striking glassworkers to the Place Gambetta, Carmaux, 1895. 149

3. Striking glassworkers leaving their union hall, October 1895. 152

4. The strike committee, October, 1895. (At center, with cigarette, Michel Aucouturier.) 156

5. Glassworkers building the Verrerie Ouvrière, Albi, 1896. 172

6. Wax models of an *équipe* of glassworkers in 1896, at the Musée de la Verrerie Ouvrière, Albi. 173

Tables

1. Population Growth in the Tarn, 1856–1876. 13

2. Number of Houses per Street on Major Streets in Carmaux, 1866–1886. 14

Tables

3. Number of Individuals per House on Major Streets in Carmaux, 1866–1886.   15
4. Population Growth in Carmaux, 1856–1896.   15
5. Daily Wage of Workers in France (Excluding Paris), 1871.   39
6. Daily Wages of Glassworkers, in Selected Departments, 1882.   40
7. Daily Wages in Selected Industries (All Departments except the Seine), 1882.   40
8. Average Daily Wages in Large Industry in the Tarn, 1882.   41
9. Average Daily Wages in Small Industry in the Tarn, 1882.   41
10. Age-Specific Death Rates of Glassworkers Dying in Carmaux, Five-Year Periods, 1876–1896.   44
11. Infant Mortality in Carmaux, 1853–1862, 1903–1912.   45
12. Number of Employees at the Verrerie Sainte Clothilde, 1871 and 1876–1887.   76
13. Number of Glassworkers Arriving in Carmaux, by Decade, 1856–1895.   76
14. Average Daily Wages at the Verrerie Sainte Clothilde, Selected Years, 1876–1887.   81
15. Average Daily Wages of Glassworkers (All Departments, except the Seine), Selected Years, 1882–1893.   82
16. Glassworker Leaders in Carmaux, 1890–1895.   95
17. Number of Votes Received in the Election to the Conseil d'Arrondissement, Canton of Carmaux, August, 1892.   133
18. Unions of Glassworkers in France, 1884–1900.   164
19. Average Daily Wages of Glassworkers and Miners in Carmaux, 1902 and 1906.   175

Figures

Appendix Tables

A. Occupations of Fathers of Glassworkers Married in Carmaux, by Decade, 1866–1905.   203
B. Birthplace of Glassworkers Married in Carmaux, by Decade, 1866–1905.   204
C. Occupations of Fathers of Glassworkers Aged 10 to 19 Years, 1876, 1891, and 1896.   205
D. Geographic Mobility of Glassworkers in Carmaux, by Decade, 1866–1895.   206

Figures

1. Map of Carmaux, canton and city.   8
2. Age structure of glassworkers in Carmaux, five-year periods, 1866–1896.   78
3. Members of the national federation of glassworkers, 1883–1900.   165
4. Members of the miners union of Carmaux, 1883–1914.   166

The Glassworkers of Carmaux

. . . je soufflais de l'aube au soir encore, toujours!
Je gonflais de ma vie la fusion vermeille,
Avec ma part de ciel je créais des contours,
Le vent de mes poumons animait les bouteilles

. . . Leur couleur était faite avec mon énergie,
Je soufflais la gaieté, les songes et l'amour . . .
-Ô bouteilles, pour posséder tout de magie
Vous me buviez mon sang! Et je soufflais toujours!

"L'Adieu du Verrier"
par Maurice Magre, 1899

Introduction

The glassworkers of Carmaux first came to my attention because they led a long strike in 1895 which was supported by the efforts of leading French socialists, among them and most outstanding, Jean Jaurès. As a result of the strike a cooperative glassworks, the Verrerie Ouvrière, was established in 1896 at Albi. I was interested less in the immediate circumstances of the strike, though it was a dramatic occasion of working-class militancy, than in its long-range implications. Here was a case of a group of unionized workers, defining themselves as socialists and acting collectively against their employer. What was the source of their "class consciousness"? Why did they strike when they did? What did socialism mean to them in the context of 1895?

It seemed to me these questions would permit a view "from below" of at least one segment of the French labor movement, whose history is traditionally written as the history of strikes, organizations, and leaders.[1] I did not want to write a history of the glassworkers' strike of 1895; instead I wanted to use that strike as a lever which would permit me to examine the strikers, to learn more about what motivated them and enabled them to act when and as they did.

To answer the questions I had asked I felt I had to know a great deal about the experiences of glassworkers over a long period of time. Having been influenced by historians of the *longue durée* (the study of long-term patterns rather than specific events) and by the works of historical demographers,[2] I began to assemble bits of information which might illuminate the patterns of glassworker experience and pinpoint changes in those patterns as well. The sources included the traditional materials of historical inquiry— newspapers; books; trade-union congresses; police, administrative, and family archives—as well as the data of the quantifier. Demographic records, particularly, became invaluable. The data collected from the quinquennial census and from civil records of marriage, birth, and death furnished information about the occupations of workers and of their fathers and sons (and, therefore, about intergenerational occupational mobility), about their birthplaces (and, therefore, about patterns of geographic mobility), and about their ages at marriage and death. Lists of witnesses at weddings and of godparents at baptisms enabled me to analyze patterns of friendship and of social intercourse. Both kinds of sources permitted the reconstruction of the lives of hundreds of glassworkers who left no written records and about whom no biographies ever were written. It would have been impossible for me to interpret the demographic data without also analyzing the written sources. I would have had no sense of context, no "feel" for the people and issues involved. But the meaning of the words I read, the underlying issues they referred to, became clearest in the light of the numerical tables.

As I developed a history of glassworkers and compared their experiences with those of Carmaux's miners, I became convinced that changes in what Remi Gossez calls "the structure of work" were the focus of my study.[3] This book, therefore, details and analyzes the experiences of artisan glassblowers as their trade was transformed by mechanization from a highly skilled art to a semiskilled operation. It is ultimately in the glassworkers' experience of occupational change that I find an explanation for the events of 1895.

Although it is a case study of a particular and probably unique craft, this book has implications beyond its immediate subject. It permits a close examination of the impact of industrialization on artisans and, precisely because it is a case study, it allows us to refine or qualify existing generalizations. The artisans who are the subject of this study were glass-bottle makers. Until the early 1880's they formed a highly skilled, closed trade. Their numbers were few compared to miners or building workers and their wages made them part of the elite of French workingmen. In one sense, they were hardly typical of the ordinary laborer or the small urban craftsman. Yet any case study would have similar limitations. No group of workmen is exactly like any other; the conditions of their trade will always be somewhat unique. What makes a trade typical or representative, however, is the fact that certain of its experiences are shared by other workers; that the reactions of its members resemble (indeed are often indistinguishable from) those of members of other trades. In this sense, the glassworkers seem to be a representative group of artisans. The introduction of certain kinds of machinery in the 1880's moved them to unionize and to strike as artisans before them had done. Many of the strikes during the July

Monarchy had involved protests against machines, for example. Furthermore, there appears to have been a high correlation between mechanization and strikes in France from 1864 to 1913.[4] In the 1890's, the glassworkers of Carmaux participated in the movement which saw an increase in labor conflicts and particularly in strikes, a proliferation of unions and national labor organizations, and the spread of socialism in the cities of France.

This case study, however, does more than substantiate once again the generalization that mechanization leads artisans to protest. Its emphasis on a specific situation and on concrete detail permits an understanding of exactly how the generalization was experienced by workingmen and it helps answer the question: *Why* did mechanization lead artisans to protest? The traditional answer to that question was that they had become proletarianized. The deflation of their status led artisans to perceive that their plight was that of other workers. They acquired class consciousness because they had become proletarians.[5] Yet the study of the glassworkers of Carmaux leads to modification, indeed revision, of this argument. As mechanization transformed glassblowing into a semiskilled trade, the glassworkers attempted to protect their economic and craft status by forming a union. They employed the language of class struggle, but it expressed specific craft concerns. The union represented a last-ditch effort by craftsmen to save their craft: an attempt to halt the process of proletarianization rather than an indication that the process was complete. When the craftsmen failed to halt the process, they abandoned the union and the craft. Artisan glassworkers did not become factory operatives, nor did their sons. Instead, new men were recruited from lower-status jobs. And they were more proletarianized but decidedly less militant than their artisan predecessors.

For the glassworkers of Carmaux there was a direct and immediate correlation between occupational changes and the form and substance of their trade union. Socialism, too, made a specific and pragmatic appeal to their immediate concerns as workers and as urban residents. An understanding of this appeal throws new light on the reasons for the success of French Marxists in winning workers' votes in the 1890's, and it points up the need for a reexamination of French socialism from the perspective of its constituents.

One of the striking aspects of the socialists' appeal involved an emphasis on urban living conditions. In Carmaux there was a definite link between the growth of the city and the growth of socialism, but not because life in the city created alienated, uprooted dissidents, nor because the incoming migrants were more prone to action. Miners and glassworkers began to settle in Carmaux in the 1890's because their work demanded it. The growth of socialism, in part, expressed a new identification of themselves as members of the municipality and it flowed from sustained contacts among workers made possible by permanent residence. Changes in working conditions and in the city made organization possible; from organization came action.

But the action of socialist glassworkers in the 1890's did not herald the dawn of a new era. The strikes and socialist political victories of 1895 did not mark a new stage in the unfolding of working-class consciousness. Instead they expressed the specific needs of a particular historical moment. For several decades after 1895 there were no strikes or unions among the glassworkers of Carmaux. From the perspective of longue durée, 1895 pinpoints yet another change, away from strikes and working-class solidarity to a period of division, disunity, and discord. Here again, a case study serves to challenge a long-held assumption about the linear evolution of working-class consciousness, an assumption often implicit in histories of the French labor movement.[6]

Carmaux became one of a few industrial centers in the predominantly agricultural department of the Tarn during the nineteenth century. Fifteen kilometers north of Albi, in the southwestern region of France, it was above all a mining town, located in the heart of a rich and extensive coal basin. The mines lay close to the town, at distances not greater than two kilometers. They were owned by the Solages family, which had exploited the natural wealth of its lands since 1752. An enterprising noble family of the type described by Robert Forster in *The Nobility of Toulouse in the Eighteenth Century*, the Solages also owned a glass factory and an iron mill, both of which used coal as fuel.[1]

Carmaux's population grew slowly in the first half of the century. It was designated a city only in 1841, when its population finally passed 2,000. Carmaux was distinguished nonetheless by its size and its commercial activity from the surrounding rural villages. Few of them boasted even a baker, although in 1851 there were six bakers in Carmaux. Furthermore, after 1844, Carmaux held a market once a month, which drew to it large numbers of peasants and established its position as a small urban center in the area. Yet compared to the Tarn's industrial cities, Carmaux was quite small, and in the first part of the century, it can be characterized only as "preindustrial." The inhabitants of

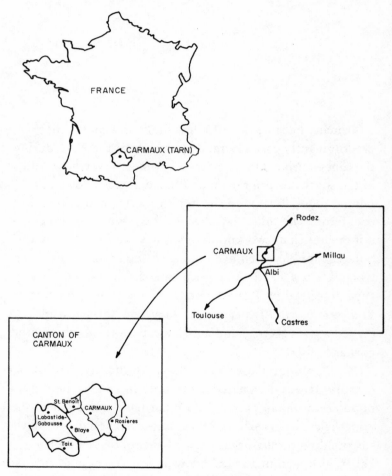

`1. Map of Carmaux, canton and city.

the textile centers of Castres and Mazamet numbered 22,062 and 10,368, respectively, in 1856. Albi, the capital city of the department, had 14,636 residents. In contrast, Carmaux listed only 3,743.[2]

If size distinguished Carmaux from Castres and Mazamet, so did appearance. Neither factories nor crowded dwellings were anywhere evident. The mines lay outside the city and their soot and grime disfigured it little. Unlike neighboring Decazeville, with its open shafts, Carmaux's coal was mined deep below the surface of the earth in closed pits. As a result, though portions of the countryside lay barren and black, the town's buildings were clean and the oppressive blackness which blanketed many another mining town was absent. In fact, it would have been difficult to guess the industry of the town merely by walking through it. Although almost half of Carmaux's male population were miners in 1851, most lived in the outlying rural sections of the city. Many of the other 500 men employed in the mines lived on farms in the rural communes contiguous to Carmaux. Whether they resided in the city or not, most miners owned their own homes and some land and they lived the lives of peasants rather than of urban workers. The crowded company towns, the *corons* of the north, had no counterpart in Carmaux.

The glassworks, too, lay outside the city in 1851. The group of buildings which comprised the Verrerie Royale was located on the grounds of the Solages's château in Blaye, the commune immediately to the west of Carmaux. The craftsmen engaged in the blowing of wine bottles lived at the château. Their assistants lived in Carmaux or the surrounding countryside.

Carmaux in 1851 consisted of a small central area of old

residential dwellings which housed a few shops and a fairly
heterogeneous assortment of people. Some miners and
small craftsmen lived side by side with shopkeepers and an
occasional farmer. The town supported sixteen tradesmen,
among them three butchers, six bakers, and a pastry-maker.
There were four inns and seven cafés. The professionals
included a doctor, two teachers, a pharmacist, and a notary.
One curé, assisted by two vicars, tended the religious affairs
of the Carmausins.[3] The most prominent buildings in the
city were the church and the town hall, which faced one
another in the main square. This square served also as the
market site on the first Friday of each month. Moving out
from the center of town, houses were fewer and farther
apart until at the edges the landscape was completely rural.

Just outside the city limits stood another prominent
building, perhaps the most significant for the residents of
Carmaux. The Solages château, surrounded by a large park,
stood aloof from the daily activities of the city. Nonetheless its proximity to the town and to the mines and glassworks, as well as its very aloofness, spoke of the controlling
influence the noble family exercised on Carmaux.

The geography of Carmaux and even the relationships of
its buildings aptly reflected the town's social structure.
Above and apart from the rest of the population were the
noble Solages. At some distance below them on the social
pyramid were a small group of large landholders. Close to
them, and often allied by family ties, were a few prominent
professionals and the Director of the Mines. (The liberal
professions accounted for 8 men in the census of 1851.) A
large area of social space separated these people from a
more numerous group which included Carmaux's 16 shopkeepers and its 125 craftsmen and journeymen (among

them a small, but distinct community of glassworkers).
Below these, but not always clearly separate were some 500
miners, most of whom were indistinguishable from the wide
peasant base on which the pyramid rested. As the town
merged with the rural countryside, so did the bulk of its
population.[4]

Whatever his formal occupation, a man's prestige as well
as his wealth derived from his ownership of land. Under the
laws of the July Monarchy officials were eligible for election only if they owned property. The members of the
Municipal Council of Carmaux in 1837 thus reported their
personal wealth in terms of revenues from their land,
although they described themselves with different occupational titles. The wealthiest man on the Council, who also
served as Mayor, was the cashier at the mines. The next
wealthiest was a businessman. The most numerous group
(six) designated themselves landowners (propriétaires), and
their fortunes ranged from 1500 to 3000 francs in revenues
annually. The doctor and two innkeepers had incomes
equal to these landholders. Two merchants ranked last with
annual incomes of 1000 francs each.[5] The Revolution of
1848 brought little change in the political influence of the
socially prominent in Carmaux. On August 13, 1848, the
town installed as its newly elected municipal council twelve
landowners, two businessmen, a doctor, a notary, and an
innkeeper. These represented many of the same families
who served on the council in 1837 and 1843. There were,
however, some new occupations represented as well. The
presence of a miner and a mason and of two small shopkeepers (a butcher and a baker) were undoubtedly the
result of the Republican introduction of universal manhood
suffrage. Nevertheless, the overwhelming majority of

council members came from the upper strata and represented landed wealth.[6]

In fact, the dominant feature of Carmaux in 1851 was
its inextricable connection with the countryside. Even
mining, the major industry of the town, was a form of
agricultural activity in this period. For the peasant-miners
who alternated labor in the fields with work in the pits
were engaged in different forms of exploitation of the
earth. The rhythm of their lives was attuned to the seasons;
they dug coal only when they were not sowing or harvesting their crops.

Symbolically and actually, the arrival of the railroad in
1864 brought industrialization to Carmaux. The Solages
company had asked for a trunk line connecting Carmaux to
Albi and Toulouse to facilitate the transport of their coal.[7]
The completion of the line coincided with a number of
other developments which dramatically altered the appearance and quiet, indeed, the very character of the town. In
1862, a new owner, Fernand Rességuier, moved the glass
works to a site near the railroad station and enlarged its
operations, thus bringing a small manufacturing establishment and its workers into the city. Although, of course, the
mines remained where they were, their operations too,
were expanded and rationalized and more and more miners
began to settle within Carmaux. As miners and glassworkers
came to the city, its population grew enormously. Between
1856 and 1876 it increased by 64 percent, a rate of growth
more than double that of any other city in the Tarn.[8]

Carmaux did not merely become a larger version of what
it had been. Its geography and appearance altered as well.
In the central areas, streets had earlier begun to be widened
and access to them improved. The main street was equip-

ped with lights in 1861.[9] Yet the more significant changes took place to the west and north of the old central city. Around the glassworks and the railroad station the glassworkers established their neighborhood. The number of houses standing on the Rue de la Gare and the Rue de la Verrerie doubled in ten years (1866–1876); the number of people living in those two streets more than doubled.[10] The average number of residents per house rose from seven in 1866 to eleven in 1876, when there were an average of three rather than two families per house. Population was denser, living quarters more crowded. A tall smoke stack exhausting fumes from the glassworks furnace, the daily sound of train brakes and of laborers loading coal and bottles, the sight of the glassworkers in their white smocks entering and leaving the factory made Carmaux's industry audible and visible.

At a considerable distance from this activity on the north side of the river, Le Cerou, the *quartier* Sainte Cécile was increasingly populated by miners, who were under pressure from their employer to move closer to the mines. Although miners still lived in individual houses, population in this

Table 1. Population Growth in the Tarn, 1856–1876

City	1856	1876	Increase (percent)
Albi	14,636	19,169	30.9
Castres	22,062	25,856	17.1
Mazamet	10,368	14,168	36.6
Carmaux	3,743	6,160	64.5

Source: André Armengaud, *Les Populations de l'Est-Aquitain au début de l'époque contemporaine* (Paris, 1961), 260.

section was more crowded than elsewhere. Sainte Cécile rapidly acquired a special identity as a miners' neighborhood and, later, as a center of working-class militancy. (In the election of 1892 more than 73 percent of its residents voted socialist, and it is still one of the few places in the country with a street named for Robespierre.) In 1889, when Carmaux's administrative designation changed from a commune in the canton of Monestiès to the head commune of the canton of Carmaux, its population numbered almost 9000. Glassworkers and miners accounted

Table 2. Number of Houses per Street on Major Streets in Carmaux, 1866–1886

Street	1866	1876	1886	Net loss or gain
Route Impériale (after 1870, Nationale)	101	107	107	+ 6
Rue de la Gare	29	52	72	+43[a]
Rue de la Verrerie	3	11	25	+22[a]
Rue Impériale (later Nationale)	16	31	24	+ 8
Rue de la Tour	71	78	49	–22[b]
Rue du Centre	27	36	36	+ 9
Cambon	31	28	27	– 4[c]
Deux Ponts	17	18	15	– 2[c]
Pont Vieux	18	15	13	– 5[c]

Source: A.M. Carmaux, Liste nominative du dénombrement de la population, 1866, 1876, 1886.
[a]Rapid growth of glassworker neighborhood in relation to other parts of the city. (Losses on the Rue de la Tour could not have been gains on either of these streets, since they were not contiguous.)
[b]Decrease of this size most likely resulted from renaming a portion of the street.
[c]May have resulted from destruction of houses or from enumerators' errors.

for more than half of its male residents. Some miners had already begun to settle in Blaye and Saint Benoît, hoping to avoid the congestion and higher prices of the city and to be able to continue farming a plot larger than the small

Table 3. Number of Individuals per House on Major Streets in Carmaux, 1866–1886

Street	1866	1876	1886
Route Impériale (after 1870, Nationale)	7	6	6
Rue de la Gare	9	10	10[a]
Rue de la Verrerie	6	13	10[b]
Rue Impériale (later Nationale)	6	6	6
Rue de la Tour	7	6	7
Rue du Centre	7	7	7
Cambon	5	6	6
Deux Ponts	6	5	5
Pont Vieux	4	5	7

Source: A.M. Carmaux, Liste nominative de population, 1866, 1876, 1886.
[a]The greater number of individuals in a house resulted *not* from a difference in house size. Most houses on all these streets comprised one or two households. *Nor* were glassworker families larger. Rather, the larger number reflects practices peculiar to glassworkers: (1) taking in boarders and (2) several families sharing one lodging.
[b]This may reflect a drop in itinerancy. There would be fewer boarders in a settling population. (See below, Chapter 4.)

Table 4. Population Growth in Carmaux, 1856–1896

1856	1876	1886	1891	1896
3743	6160	8059	9531	9993

Source: A.M. Carmaux, Liste nominative de population, 1856–1896.

garden typical of the miner's holding in the city of
Carmaux.[11] The growth of population, as well as the decline
of its self-sufficient rural inhabitants, was reflected in the
lists of tradesmen. In 1889, Carmaux had twenty-three
grocers and eleven butchers (four times as many as in 1851).
There were twenty-six bakers (compared to six in 1851),
but only two pastry-makers, evidence that bread was still
the staple in a workingman's diet and that cakes were a
luxury for the rich. The shops of seventeen tailors and
twelve hairdressers, however, told of the expanded consumer needs and tastes of workers, as well as of an increase
in middle-class residents.[12]

Carmaux's population not only had grown, a subtle shift
in social values had occurred as well. The old hierarchy
remained: the shape, as it were, of social structure still
resembled a pyramid. But land was less important as a
source of status and wealth than was a man's occupation.
In part this stemmed from changes in national values. By
the 1880's, fortunes had been made in industrial enterprises
and the possession of wealth was more important than its
source. In addition, universal suffrage meant that political
influence and power were no longer the preserve of those
who owned large tracts of land. Yet the changes in
Carmaux also had purely local origins in the growth of
industry and of the city itself. Inextricably a part of the
national political and economic organization, the local experience, nonetheless, was the context within which Carmaux's
residents defined their values and from which notions of
social status derived their meaning.

Their historic position as the town notables, as well as
their great wealth, placed the Solages at the pinnacle of
the social hierarchy. But increasingly, the family's power

and prominence rested on its control of the mines. The other leading figure in Carmaux was the owner of the glassworks, Fernand Rességuier. The next level now included not only landowners and professionals but several of the higher-level administrative personnel at the mines and glassworks. Between these and the shopkeepers and craftsmen came a new group of white-collar employees in the mining and glassworking companies—engineers, supervisors, salesmen, and office managers. Miners, still the bulk of the town's population, were now urban workers higher in status than peasants, though still subordinate to most other skilled workers.

By 1890, then, position in the social hierarchy was almost exclusively a function of one's work in the city. The membership of the Municipal Council in 1888 reflected this development as well as the democratizing of the city government. Of its twenty-three members, only two described themselves as landowners. The rest held a variety of positions, among them two hotelkeepers, three bakers, a businessman, a surveyor, a notary, a shoemaker, a watchmaker, a miner, and two glassworkers.[13] In 1890 Carmaux was still a relatively small but distinctly industrial city. In 1841 it had had a population density of 153 inhabitants per square kilometer. By 1891, Carmaux resembled many another industrial town with 686 inhabitants per square kilometer. (In 1911, the figure rose still higher, to 791 per square kilometer.)[14] In one sense the growth of Carmaux merely reflected the growth of its industry. The city was the setting for a number of purely industrial developments, a place to which glassworkers and miners came in order to work. Yet the development of industry and the influx of large numbers of workers into Carmaux altered the city itself. An altered city meant that the quality and style of life of Carmaux's inhabitants, as well as their relationships to one another, were different in 1890 from what they had been in 1851. This was so not only because of changes in the nature of their work but because physical conditions were different: streets were more crowded, houses closer together, and people more aware of one another. These conditions modified the perception of the city by miners and glassworkers and likewise their perception of their own relationship to it. And as industrial growth stimulated commercial activity and urban growth, urban growth affected the living conditions and political attitudes of workers. The growth of Carmaux was not merely the locus for, nor the sole cause of, the development of class consciousness among Carmaux's workers. Rather, it was an inextricable part of the process of economic, social, and political change which is detailed in the remainder of this book.

The Craft of the Glassworker
2

"Un métier artisanal d'élite"

From the founding of the glassworks at Carmaux in 1754 until the early 1880's, the craft practiced by the glassworkers of Carmaux remained essentially unaltered. Despite a change in management in 1856, a subsequent expansion of the factory, and some modifications of traditional arrangements, glassworkers experienced no major disruptions of the organization of their work nor of the style of their lives.

The distinguishing characteristic of most French glassworkers during these years was that they were highly skilled workers who maintained the artisanal standards and traditions of their trade within a system of capitalist manufacture. They were able to do so because the manufacture of glass bottles depended on their skill. Although they worked for wages in the shops of employers who owned the means of production, glassblowers nonetheless controlled most aspects of their trade. They alone managed the hiring and training of apprentices and thereby regulated the labor supply. They also set the standards for the quality of their product and the conditions of their work. In addition, the possession of skill and the control of its transmission allowed glassworkers to maintain regular and relatively high wages, to enjoy a social position higher than that of most other workers, and to rest secure about their own occupational futures as well as about those of their sons.[1] In fact, if wages are the determining standard, glassworkers were an elite among French workers. During most of the nineteenth century they earned more than most other workers in France. Yet high wages did not alone define the superior status of French glassworkers. Rather, their higher level of wages was but one of the distinguishing characteristics of the members of the fraternity of craftsmen whose work and life-style set them apart from other workers in France. A subprefect characterized them well in 1848 when he described glassworkers as "honest and skilled workers, accustomed to ease by their high wages . . . in general [they are] elite workers."[2]

Whether one begins at the beginning—in 1754 with the founding of the Verrerie Royale de Carmaux by the Chevalier de Solages—or, more than a century later, in 1862 when Fernand Rességuier reopened the enlarged (and renamed) Verrerie Sainte Clothilde, one finds artisan glassblowers producing dark bottles for wine in essentially the same fashion.

The beginning was elaborate and dramatic. In an unusually long entry in his parish register, the curé of Carmaux detailed the baptism of La Verrerie on April 20, 1754. Assisted by two other priests, the curé in surplice and violet hat raised the cross and began his tour, chanting the *Veni Creator* as he walked. When he arrived at the furnace he sang a psalm and then lit its first fire. As the flames soared, his voice rang out the *Te Deum*. The curé then proceeded to sanctify a house adjacent to the glassworks which was to lodge the workers. Two days later a solemn mass was sung asking God's blessing for the new enterprise of the Chevalier de Solages.[3]

The new glassworks adjoined the château of its owner, Gabriel de Solages, a son of Carmaux's leading noble family. It consisted of "a building which housed two furnaces [although only one was operated at a time], four store-rooms for the bottles, a room for the ashes, one for the sand, one for the earth." There were several other shops in which stones were ground, and where blacksmiths and carpenters worked. A separate building housed the workers.[4] A fire, fueled by coal from the Solages's mines melted the constituents of the glass which had been placed in crucibles (or *pots*) in the furnace. Teams of four glass-workers stood at various openings in the furnace in which the crucibles were placed. The number of teams depended on the number of such openings in the furnace. In 1754, there were four such places at the Verrerie Royale, which meant that five teams (four and one relay to replace ill or absent workers) were employed. From 1758 until 1849 these twenty glassworkers increased production from 200,000 to 600,000 bottles a year. The bottles were sold in Montauban, Toulouse, and Bordeaux.[5]

In 1853, in a matter-of-fact business contract, written by lawyers without the blessing of the local priest, the Solageses transformed their family-owned mines into a corporation and then in 1856 rented the glassworks to an enterprising bottle merchant from Toulouse, M. Fernand Rességuier. (Rességuier had bought the factory from Solages by 1862.) Rességuier maintained marginal production at the old factory while he began construction of a new building near the site of the railway station. The new glassworks opened in 1862. It was a large rectangular building, housing a single furnace. Unlike his noble predecessors, the bourgeois Rességuier expanded his enterprise as rapidly as he could. In 1875 he had six furnaces operating and 250 workers employed. By 1882, some 300 workers produced 21,000 bottles a day, twice as many as had been produced ten years earlier and thirty times as many as were blown in 1758.[6]

The absence of ceremony is not the only difference between 1754 and 1862. Whereas the Solages family considered the glassworks secondary to its major enterprise of coal mining, Rességuier sought to expand the profits and production of glassmaking, his sole source of income. The Solageses employed the same numbers of workers and increased production only gradually over a century, while Rességuier's first twenty years were marked by unprecedented expansion. In 1754, Solages provided lodging and food for his glassworkers in accordance with the custom then prevailing. Overall, the noble family's reign seems to have been marked by a certain paternalism: retired glassworkers received pensions, although no contract stipulated this and no association existed to enforce it. Furthermore, widows of glassworkers were often employed in the glassworks or in the household of the Marquis.[7] Rességuier's workers, on the other hand, rented their dwellings. Although no records of his company survive to be compared with the Solages archives, it can be assumed that the size of Rességuier's workforce made employer-employee relations more impersonal than they had been before. In the long run, Rességuier's drive for increased profits would lead him

to mechanize production, but until 1883 he merely enlarged and expanded his factory without altering the
traditional organization of work.

At the Verrerie Royale and the Verrerie Sainte Clothilde
work centered around the furnace, a large brick structure
with several windowlike openings. In each opening was a
crucible within which the constituents of glass were heated
until they became molten. A team of glassworkers gathered
near each opening of the furnace. Each team represented a
hierarchy of skill, consisting of a master (*souffleur*), two
apprentices (*grand garçon* and *gamin* or *petit garçon*—the
designations reflecting age as well as ability)—and served by
a bottle carrier (*porteur*). Only the souffleur, the grand
garçon, and the gamin were called glassworkers (*verriers*);
everyone else was referred to either according to the task
he performed or as a worker at the glassworks (an *ouvrier à
la verrerie*). The bottle carrier was usually the young son of
a glassworker, about nine or ten years old. He brought the
finished bottles to baths for gradual cooling and then to the
arrangeur who stacked and sorted them. By the age of
twelve or thirteen, he began his technical apprenticeship.
Apprentices at both stages had to prepare the instruments
and the glass. The younger gamins cleaned the iron-blowing
pipe (*la canne*) and heated it. The older grands garçons
adjusted the size of the opening at the end of the pipe and
also skimmed the molten glass to remove small particles of
sand or stone which would result in imperfections in the
finished bottles. In addition, the apprentices participated
in the blowing of bottles. The gamin placed the heated tube
through an opening in the side of the furnace into a
crucible full of molten glass. This task, termed "the gather-

Plate I.
Figure 1. Interior of a glassworks with a coal-burning furnace at the center.
Figure 2. *Gamin.*
a) *gamin* gathering glass b) *canne* (blowing tube)
c) opening from which glass is taken

24

Plate II.

Figure 1. Worker cooling the tube.
a) tube b) tub of water in which blowing tube is cooled
c) iron bar to support tube d) iron surface (*marbre*) on which glass is turned
e) stone supporting the marbre

Figure 2. *Grand garçon* shaping glass.
a) tube b) inflated glass (*la paraison*) c) *marbre* d) support of *marbre*
e) mold in which bottles are blown

25

Plate III.
Figure 1. Forming the neck of the bottle.
a) tube b) inflated glass c) *marbre* d) iron bar to support tube
Figure 2. *Grand garçon* inflating glass until it takes the shape of an egg.
a) tube b) glass c) bar to support tube d) *marbre*
e) *marbre* support
f) mold for bottle

26

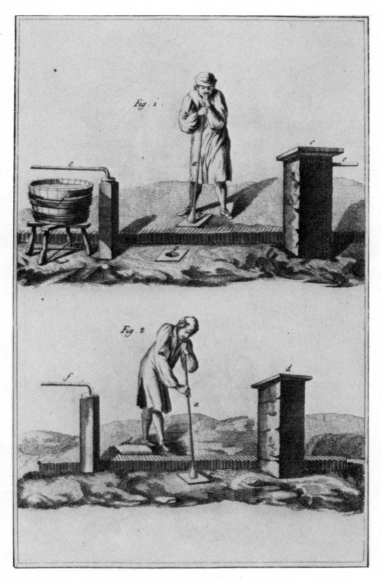

Plate IV.
Figure 1. *Souffleur* inflating glass before putting it into mold.
a) tube b) bottle c) mold
Figure 2. *Souffleur* blowing bottle in mold.
a) tube b) bottle c) mold d) *marbre*
e) *marbre* support
f) tube support

27

Plate V.

Figure 1. *Souffleur* shaping bottom of bottle.

a) tube b) iron tool (*mollette*) c) bottom of bottle d) *marbre* e) mold

Figure 2. *Souffleur* rolling bottle on *marbre* to shape it.

a) tube b) bottle c) *marbre* d) *marbre* support

Figure 3. *Souffleur* preparing to shape bottle neck.

a) tube b) bottle c) tube support d) wall to protect worker from heat

Plate VI.

Figure 1. *Souffleur* making neck of bottle.
a) tube b) bottle g) wall to protect worker from heat

Figure 2. Making the neck of the bottle.
a) tube resting on arms of bench b) bottle c) pliers used to form neck d) bench

Figure 3. Pliers.
a) handle b) blade c) side which fits into first blade

29

Plate VII.

Figure 1. *Porteur* putting finished bottle in annealing furnace.
a) annealing furnace   c) heating grille   e) bottle   g) vents
Figure 2. *Gamin* scraping glass off tube which has been used to blow a bottle.
a) tube   b) glass attached to tube   c) iron hammer to remove glass   d) base
e) container for broken glass pieces
Figure 3. Hammer.
a) head   b) handle
Figure 4. Iron tool used to make the bottom of the bottle.

ing of the glass," although not as demanding as that of his superiors, required that the young boy acquire a certain dexterity:

He plunges the end of the tube about three inches into the glass. He withdraws the tube and lets the glass cool a bit . . . all the while turning the tube to roll the glass around it, without dropping any of the glass. Then he returns the tube to the crucible and repeats the operation. He does this four, five or six times, depending on whether the glass is hard or soft. Then the grand garçon takes it and gathers the last bit of glass.[8]

The grand garçon usually (but sometimes the souffleur himself) then shaped the glass and began to blow the bottle. It took speed, accuracy, and a great deal of coordination to begin inflating the glass, to "make it appear" as the operation was called:

He rests the part of the glass which is nearer to his hand on the sharp edge of the left side of an iron slab; leans his body to the right and turns the tube while pulling it towards himself, thus flattening the glass along the tube. He then rests the glass on the flat surface without leaning his body in any direction; he then tilts the tube and his body down and forward, gently pressing the end of the tube where the glass is against the slab, rolls the flattened glass around the tube and raises it straight up. He rests the glass against the slab, puts the tube to his mouth, holding his right hand near his mouth, his left outstretched. He blows as he turns the tube and slowly inflates the glass until it takes the shape of an egg . . . [9]

This step completed, the grand garçon then took the tube to the furnace and turned it rapidly to reheat the glass. When the glass was hot enough he handed the pipe to the souffleur, who alone was qualified to finish the process.

The master . . . then blows until he considers it ready to be put into the mold. When he puts it there he pushes it against the bottom of the mold and blows, turning the tube constantly until he sees the bottle shaped as he wants it. Then he withdraws it from the mold and shakes it to shape the bottom.[10]

Having shaped the bottle, the souffleur in one motion removed it from the pipe and began to make the rim.

He rests the tube in a groove, holding it in his left hand, while he takes a smaller tube in his right. He plunges the end of the smaller tube into the crucible, withdraws it and attaches a bit of glass to the top of the bottle, turning the tube so that a thin strip of glass is attached to the top of the bottle. He pulls back this tube quickly so that the remaining glass breaks off itself. He reheats the mouth of the bottle, carries it to the bench, sits down, takes an iron tool and with its flat side, strikes the mouth once or twice.[11]

With another tool he rounded off the mouth. The finished bottle was then passed to the grand garçon who passed it to the porteur who took it to the annealing furnace.

A team usually produced fifty-six bottles in a twelve-hour day, or about five bottles an hour. But if it took ten or twelve minutes to blow a bottle, it took years to train a man to blow one. Apprentices only gradually developed the ability to judge the proper temperature and state of the glass, and it took some years of practice to coordinate the rapid and accurately timed motions required to produce a perfectly shaped bottle. Each stage of apprenticeship lasted about five years, which meant that an apprentice became a souffleur in his early twenties, about the time he became a man.[12]

The team was the crucial unit of relationship for glassworkers. The souffleur maintained the pace and quality of work, he trained, hired, and fired apprentices, and determined their wages and the terms of their promotion. The personnel of a team usually did not change for several years, permitting the development of close working relationships. Often, too, the apprentices were the souffleur's sons. Familial relationships thus reflected and reinforced the hierarchy of work and skill. The organization of work in small teams must have mitigated the effects of the impersonality of Rességuier's administration. Only the souffleurs who dealt directly with their employer may have experienced increasing impersonality as the factory grew. Yet as long as their employer depended upon their skills, the souffleurs maintained the essential controls over those under them and over conditions and standards of production that their ancestors had enjoyed a century earlier.

In addition, the method by which glass was prepared and the rhythm of work continued under Rességuier as it had been under the Solageses. Molten glass was prepared for twelve hours (from noon until midnight) in coal-heated furnaces. The glassworkers blew bottles during the coolest part of the day, from midnight until noon. The factory still employed a number of skilled and unskilled auxiliary workers who assisted in the production of bottles, working in small shops or in the courtyard of the building. Among the skilled auxiliaries were the stokers, who maintained the furnace at an even temperature, and the blacksmiths and the potters, who prepared and mended the molds and crucibles. Highly paid clerks supervised the warehouses

where bottles were counted, packed, and stored. Unskilled
laborers, including women, washed and crushed the sand,
potash, and other constituents of the glass, sorted, stacked,
and packed bottles, and carried water and wine to the ever-
thirsty blowers. Only improvements in ventilation, which
drew the coal fumes out of the workshop more rapidly, and
the increased scale of production would have surprised
Carmaux's first glassblowers had they come to work for
Rességuier in 1862.[13]

Even the glassworker's economic relationship with his
employer had not changed fundamentally. Glassworkers
had always worked for wages in Carmaux under Rességuier,
as under Solages. The old method of payment changed in
the nineteenth century, but while the Solages family still
managed the glassworks. In the eighteenth century and at
least until 1817, the sum paid the souffleur (or "Messieur
l'ouvrier en bouteilles," as the records designated him)
included the wages of his apprentices, and it was paid for
the duration of the work season (or campagne), which
usually lasted six months. By 1832, this practice was
replaced by bimonthly payments to the souffleurs. By the
year 1837–38, yet another modification had occurred:
Solages paid all categories of glassworkers directly every
fifteen days.[14] Rességuier continued this practice. Moreover, glassworkers were paid in 1754 and in 1882 according to the number of bottles blown each day. They
had the right to maintain standards of quality by breaking
imperfect bottles and they were compensated for a specified number of these "rejects."

As they controlled the quality of their products, the
glassworkers controlled entry into their craft. In its origins,
glassblowing was a trade restricted to nobles; in fact it was

one of the few trades they could enter without losing status.
By 1754, though nobles retained sole rights to direct glassworks, the blowers themselves were not usually of noble
blood.[15] Yet they informally enforced the restrictions
which once had the backing of royal authority. Their
monopoly of skill meant not only that glassworkers could
train apprentices but that they could select their pupils as
well. In this manner glassworkers passed their skills to their
sons, the way rich men willed property to theirs. "To be
admitted to work in a glassworks," wrote an official at
Aniche in 1863, "it is necessary to be 'of the blood', that is
to be the son of a glassworker."[16]

Since skill is an intangible form of property, there are no
records of inheritance to document the assertion that
glassworker fathers looked upon their skills as security for
themselves and as a legacy for their sons. The continuity of
occupation from generation to generation is documented,
nevertheless, in company records and in censuses and
records of marriage, birth, and death. The marriage acts of
glassworkers in Carmaux clearly indicate that glassworker
fathers brought their sons into the craft. All of the first
glassworkers in Carmaux were sons of glassworkers, according to the records kept by the curé in his parish register.[17]
In addition, company records show that in 1817, three of
the four souffleurs employed at the Verrerie Royale were
sons of glassworkers who had come to Carmaux in the
1760's.[18] Although many more grands garçons were trained
between 1754 and 1817, only the sons of the master
craftsmen stayed to inherit their fathers' positions. Between
1793 and 1850, twenty glassworkers were married in
Carmaux; eight (or 40 percent) were sons of glassworkers.[19]
In the first decades of Rességuier's administration, the

number dropped noticeably; only 11 percent of those glassworkers married between 1866–1875 were sons of glassworkers. (See Table A, appendix.) This drop can be
explained by the fact that Rességuier had to recruit workers
as rapidly as possible and so admitted as apprentices many
more sons of local workers than he would in the future.
(The local origins are indicated by the fact that 40 percent
of glassworkers married during the decade 1866–1875 came
from the Tarn, whereas only 9 percent of those married in
the following decade would come from the Tarn.) (See
Table B, appendix.) In addition, many of the first glassworkers to arrive in the 1860's were already married. Their
backgrounds do not therefore show up in calculations based
on marriage acts. In the decade 1876–1885 the workforce
at Carmaux was more representative of past and prevailing
patterns in the craft: 40 percent of those glassworkers
married were sons of glassworkers.

  The censuses provide additional verification of the
pattern. Household heads who listed their occupations as
glassworker and who had sons over eleven years old invariably gave their sons' occupations as glassworker as well.
In 1876, 55 percent of those glassworkers aged ten to
nineteen were sons of glassworkers living with their fathers.
(See Table C, appendix.) If the family was present for more
than one census, its sons' occupations would appear as
glassworker as soon as the boys came of age. Sometimes,
too, the boys worked before they were legally permitted
to. A child labor inspector found that at least 50 of the 250
workers at the Verrerie Sainte Clothilde in 1875 were
under twelve. Almost all were the children of glassworkers,
acting as porteurs or gamins as their fathers had before
them.[20]

Nevertheless, not all glassworkers were sons of glassworkers. During most of the period from 1758 to 1880
grape cultivation for wine production increased, thereby
creating additional demand for bottles and offering new
opportunities for young men to enter the craft. In the early
period, the sons of highly paid skilled auxiliary workers at
the glassworks most frequently became glassworkers.
Advance was more difficult for them than for sons of glassblowers and usually involved many more steps. They began
at an early age doing odd jobs in the shops assisting their
fathers and glassworkers, carrying water, grinding and
cleaning sand. The move from *porteur de cour* to *porteur
de relai* (from the outer yards to an équipe) came after
three years for one Valery, *fils*. And he was sixteen when
he began the work usually given to eight- to ten-year-old
sons of glassworkers. Similarly, Raymond Maurel, son of a
laborer who had worked at the Verrerie Royale at least
since 1810, himself worked as a laborer for nineteen years
before qualifying as a gamin. In the same period of time,
however, the son of the master smelter (the most highly
paid position after the souffleur) moved from laborer to
relief souffleur.

This kind of advance usually was possible for only one of
an auxiliary's sons, though all his sons might serve at the
glassworks in some capacity. The importance and predom-
inance of family connections was indicated by the pay lists
of the glassworkers which referred to a person's place in
his family rather than to his name. Thus, Boyer, *père*; Boyer,
fils aîné; Boyer, *fils cadet*; Boyer, *le petit*, referred to the
family of master smelter, Joseph Boyer, whose oldest son,
Joseph, eventually became a souffleur. Joseph Boyer served
at the Verrerie Royale for at least thirty years (from 1810

37

to 1840), and his descendents continued to serve as glassworkers until the end of the century. In the decade 1830–1840, though the time was somewhat lessened, the pattern remained the same; only one son of a craftsman usually became a souffleur. The blacksmith, Paliès, appeared on pay lists first in 1835. His oldest son was listed as "his father's assistant" and then five years later simply as "blacksmith." A younger son was a mason; the youngest began as a gamin in 1838.[21]

Well into the nineteenth century the sons of workingmen in fairly stable and well-rewarded economic positions wanted to become glassworkers, but relatively few succeeded in entering the tightly controlled craft. Their aspirations were well founded, for glassmaking was a prestigious craft which offered high wages as well as a special social status. Warren Scoville estimates that during the eighteenth century "the net wages of most blowers probably ranged from 600 to 750 livres a year." This was considerably higher than other independent craftsmen such as carpenters, masons, and painters, who each earned an average of 250 livres a year.[22] The superiority of glassworker wages continued into the nineteenth century. Whereas small craftsmen earned a maximum of four francs a day in 1871, glassworkers earned as much as twelve francs daily, their apprentices as much as five francs a day.[23]

The more extensive figures for 1882 indicate that glassworkers were among the highest paid workers in large and small industries in France, earning a maximum of 12 francs as compared to the next highest earners—cotton weavers, who made a maximum daily wage of 8 francs. Even in departments where their earnings were lower than the national maximum of 12 francs, glassworkers remained high on the lists of well-paid workers, with an average daily wage of 5 to 6 francs. This amounted to at least double the average wage of most other independent craftsmen or industrial workers.[24] Glassworkers in Carmaux earned more than their fellow craftsmen did elsewhere and from three to four times as much as any other workers in the Tarn. And glassworker apprentices under twenty-one received wages higher than their elders in other trades. The contrast with Carmaux's miners was, perhaps, most striking of all. In 1882 a souffleur at the Verrerie Sainte Clothilde earned about 250 francs a month, and he worked eleven hours a day. A miner in that year worked eight hours a day and earned an average of 85 francs a month. Grands garçons and gamins earned 40 to 50 francs more a month than all categories of miners. The only employees at the mines whose pay equaled the glassworkers were the supervisors and white-collar workers.[25] As late as 1892, glassworkers were conscious of their economic superiority to other

Table 5. Daily Wage of Workers in France (Excluding Paris), 1871 (Francs)

Worker	Average	Maximum	Minimum
Carpenter	2.50	3.00	2.25
Hatmaker	3.25	4.00	2.25
Printer	2.75	3.00	2.50
Painter	2.75	3.00	2.50
Mason	3.00	3.50	2.25
Glassworker (Tarn only), 1876[a]	—	12.00	5.00

Source: Statistique de la France, *Statistique annuelle*, 1871.
[a]A.D. Tarn, X M 3 3.

Table 6. Daily Wages of Glassworkers,[a] in Selected Departments, 1882 (Francs)

Department	Men (over 21)
Tarn	12.00
Pas-de-Calais	10.00
Loire	6.25
Rhône	5.50
Mean for all departments	5.27

Source: Statistique annuelle, 1882.
[a] Includes verre et cristaux.

Table 7. Daily Wages in Selected Industries (All Departments except the Seine), 1882 (Francs)

Industry	Men (over 21)			Minors (15–21)		
	Minimum	Maximum	Mean	Minimum	Maximum	Mean
Glass	2.75	12.00	5.27	1.50	5.00	3.08
Cotton (weaving)	2.00	8.00	3.36	1.25	3.50	2.16
Dyeing (textile)	2.25	6.00	3.44	0.80	3.50	2.28
Foods	2.00– 3.25	4.90– 5.00	3.36– 3.80	2.00	4.00– 3.25	2.84

Source: Statistique annuelle, 1882 (This list contains only the four highest-paying of all those industries listed).

Table 8. Average Daily Wages in Large Industry in the Tarn, 1882
(Francs, Centimes)

Industry	Workers over 21	Minors ages 15–21
Tile and brick	3.00	2.00
Crockery and porcelain	3.00	2.50
Tanning	3.50	2.50
Wool spinning	2.75	2.00
Felt hatmaking	4.00	2.50
Glass (bottles)	12.00	5.00
Mines[a]		
(*piqueurs, mineurs*)	3.50	—

Source: *Statistique annuelle*, 1882.
[a]A.D. Tarn, IV M 2 68.

Table 9. Average Daily Wages in Small Industry in the Tarn, 1882
(Francs, Centimes)

Industry	Mean	Maximum	Minimum
Carpenter	3.00	3.75	2.50
Mason	2.85	3.25	2.65
Joiners	3.00	3.25	2.50
Painters (building)	3.50	4.50	3.00

Source: *Statistique annuelle*, 1882.

workers: "outside of the craft we cannot count on the support of other workers," warned a glassworker, "because we earn too much money and in relation to them we are privileged."[26]

With their higher wages the glassworkers were able to lead a somewhat more refined life than the miners. While the miners maintained gardens, living largely self-sufficiently and modestly as peasants, the glassworkers were completely dependent on local shops for their food. As a result, their wives had a more comfortable existence and were often referred to as "bourgeois" by miners' wives. Although their levels of comfort were not usually comparable to those of the middle classes, glassworker wives did have more money to spend and fewer chores to perform. Though neither wives of miners nor glassworkers usually had formal occupations in Carmaux before 1890, miners' wives tended crops and performed many more farm duties than did glassworkers' wives.

In addition to the fact that they simply had more money to spend, glassworkers had expensive tastes because of the "delicacy of their physical conditions."[27] Not only did they suffer from various lung diseases, but their taste buds were often damaged by the heat of the molten glass. Moreover, the intense heat of the furnace made them constantly thirsty, and the one duty of a glassworker's wife associated with her husband's work was to bring fresh supplies of water and wine to him at the factory. Yet another health hazard stemmed from the fact that the pipe through which bottles were blown touched several mouths in succession, thereby increasing the frequency of epidemics of serious illnesses.[28] Thus, although the lives of glassworkers were materially more comfortable than those of miners, they were also shorter and more precarious, despite the frequency of accidents and the occupational diseases customarily associated with mining. Although the average age of death of miners was almost forty-two in 1853–1862,[29] it was thirty-four for glassworkers in 1866–1875. Average age statistics are dubious measures, however, since they make no allowances for differences in age structures in a population, but they are the only ones available for purposes of contrast. Age-specific death rates are more exact, and although they could only be calculated for glassworkers, they give some indication of the relatively high frequency of deaths among young men. Glassworkers considered themselves old men at forty and the high rate of death in the forty–forty-four age group, especially, seems to document their belief.

High rates of infant mortality were also associated with glassworkers, more than with miners or with the overall experience of Carmaux. Though miners had an infant mortality rate of 197/000 in 1853–1862, glassworkers had a rate of 250/000 in 1866–1875. The overall infant mortality rate for Carmaux was 187/000.[30] Usually, high rates of infant mortality are associated with poverty, and the high rate for glassworkers at first seems at odds with their greater material comforts. It may, however, reflect other more difficult aspects of their lives. Not only were they an urban population exposed to the less sanitary conditions and greater danger of epidemics of industrial cities but they moved frequently, thereby exposing infants to greater instability of environment and greater risks of illness. There were other variations in the demographic patterns of glassworkers and miners. Glassworkers tended to marry at a slightly younger age and, partly as a result of higher infant

Table 10. Age-Specific Death Rates of Glassworkers Dying in Carmaux Five-Year Periods, 1876–1896 (Percent) (Average Number of Deaths in Age Group over Five-Year Period per 1000 Glassworkers in That Age Group in the Census)

| Census year | Age | | | | | | | | Five-year average of deaths |
	15-19	20-24	25-29	30-34	35-39	40-44	45-49	over 50	
1876	—	11.7	—	14.2	—	33.3	—	—	3
1881	—	—	11.1	—	28.5	36.3	—	50.0	8
1886	—	14.2	6.0	23.0	10.0	25.0	—	26.6	10
1891	3.7	8.8	24.4	—	5.6	26.0	20.0	20.0	17
1896	—	28.0	4.2	10.5	5.0	—	22.2	43.4	18

Source: A.M. Carmaux, Actes de Décès, 1876–1900.
Note: These figures are very crude (1) because of the relatively small number of glassworkers in Carmaux and (2) because of high rates of geographic mobility, which lessened the chances of a glassworker's dying in the city.

mortality, to have smaller families than miners.[31] Miners
had an average household size of four children in the 1850's
and 60's, whereas a glassworker's household had an average
of only two children. The smaller size of their families,
whatever the reason, may have contributed to the glassworkers' economic and social superiority.

Some information on the social position of glassworkers
can be gleaned from early parish records. In the parish
register of Carmaux from 1754 to 1789, glassworkers'
names are distinguished from other workers' by the prefix
Sieur. Only doctors, lawyers, and nobility received higher
esteem in the register; their names were always prefixed by
Monsieur. Bourgeois, tax inspector, merchant, and glassworker ranked equally in receiving the appellation Sieur.
Most other craftsmen—carpenters, blacksmiths, masons,
shoemakers, tailors, millers—as well as miners, common
laborers, and peasants were referred to merely by name.[32]

The standing of master glassblowers is documented in
early political as well as civil records. Those masters who

Table 11. Infant Mortality in Carmaux 1853–1862, 1903–1912
(Deaths Age 0–1 per 1000 Births)

Years	Glassworkers	Miners	Tarn
1853–1862	250[a]	197	187
1903–1912	208[b]	155.3	117.5

Sources: A.M. Carmaux, Actes de Décès, 1866–1875, 1896–1905 (for
glassworkers); Rolande Trempé, *Les Mineurs de Carmaux* (Paris, 1971), 316
(for miners); H. Viguier, *Evolution démographique dans le département du
Tarn depuis le début du XIXe siècle* (Albi, 1950), 143 (for the Tarn).
[a] 1866–1875 (in 1853–1862, there were too few cases for accurate calculation).
[b] 1896–1905.

45

settled in Carmaux usually bought land and often attained political office. The first electoral list for Carmaux established during the Revolution in March, 1790, was based on property qualifications. To vote one had to pay taxes equivalent to three days' labor. To run for office one's taxes had to equal ten days labor. (The value of a day of labor was set at one livre.) The first list included seven glassworkers. On November 15, 1790, Jacques Chappa, père, a glassworker who had arrived in Carmaux from Verdun in 1760, was elected a notable and a municipal officer. In 1796, as the oldest citizen in Carmaux, he was made honorary president of the provisional bureau. His son, Jacques, also a glassworker, was executive commissioner of the Directory in 1795 and was made president of the Bureau as well as of the Municipal Council in 1796.[33] During the Revolution their property holdings qualified most glassblowers as active citizens in periods of restricted franchise. And from 1834 until 1848, at least one glassblower, who listed his occupation as "glassworker-property-holder" served on the Municipal Council, whose members were predominantly landowners, professionals, and merchants.

Despite the fact that these examples indicate something of the prestige accorded a glassworker, as well as his potential (if not actual) landed wealth, they are not typical of the political experiences of most glassworkers. Few glassworkers remained in Carmaux (or for that matter in any town) long enough to acquire property or political office. High rates of geographic mobility characterized glassworkers at least as early as the seventeenth century. According to Scoville, in the seventeenth and eighteenth centuries "glassworkers were geographically more mobile than most

French workmen." And he cites a number of attempts by employers seeking state aid to prevent the migration of their employees. Royal orders from 1694 to 1785 threatened fines and even corporal punishment for deserting glassworkers; but repeated requests by owners of glass factories for new legislation seem to indicate that glassworkers defied the king and continued to move.[34] Evidence from Carmaux documents the national pattern. None of the first five souffleurs in Carmaux in 1754, nor their children, still lived in Carmaux in 1790. All of them left the town before they died, since neither their own deaths nor those of their children were recorded in the curé's register. In fact, most of the five probably left before 1763, since several new masters were listed as arriving in that year.[35]

Pay lists for the Verrerie Royale exist for 1810–1816 and for 1835–1840. These too, though an incomplete record, make it possible to determine the duration of a glassworker's stay in Carmaux. Of the eleven glassworkers working at the Solages's shops in 1810–1816 only five remained in 1835–1840. In other words, within two decades, more than 55 percent of Solages's craftsmen departed for other towns.[36] The mobility of glassworkers was not part of a formal craft practice: no *Tour de France* was required of a young apprentice. In part the mobility was a function of the physical setup of a glass factory. The number of positions for souffleurs depended on the number of openings in the furnace of the glassworks. Since more grands garçons completed their training than could be employed as souffleurs, newly trained souffleurs often moved to other regions in search of work. In Carmaux in the eighteenth and early nineteenth centuries, the master's tenure averaged twenty-five years—longer than the fifteen years' apprenticeship then required of a young man. For the most part, grands garçons whose fathers were masters in Carmaux remained there. The others left town.[37] In addition, a glassworks usually closed down for several months during the summer in order to repair its furnace. Often, during this period of *four mort*, glassworkers sought positions at other factories. These factors were compounded in the nineteenth century when, as the bottle industry expanded rapidly, the demand for skilled glassworkers exceeded the supply. Experienced souffleurs as well as newly promoted ones went from glassworks to glassworks seeking new opportunities, higher wages, and better conditions for themselves and their sons. (The attraction of higher wages alone cannot account for the glassworkers' geographic mobility since, despite the fact that the glassworkers at Carmaux remained better paid than anywhere else in France from 1862 to 1882, the population turnover was as high at the Verrerie Sainte Clothilde as at any other glassworks. Neither did high rates of mobility serve to equalize wages.)

Although there are no pay records for the period after 1862, censuses and civil records permit a thorough reconstruction of patterns of geographic mobility for the glassworkers of Carmaux. The marriage acts show that most recruits to the Verrerie Sainte Clothilde came from other departments. Theirs was not a regional migration either, for most originated in departments which were not contiguous to the Tarn. The figures for 1876–1885 are most striking: only 9 percent of the glassworkers married were born in the Tarn, while 90 percent were born in other departments, most of which were many kilometers from Carmaux. (See Table B, appendix.) An examination of the censuses also

48

reveals an extremely high turnover in the glassworker population. Most glassworkers were listed in only one census, indicating a stay of fewer than five years. Even when glassworkers who died are subtracted from the numbers departing and when calculations are made for ten-year periods, the figures do not change substantially. (see Table D, appendix.) Sixty-five percent of the glassworkers arriving in Carmaux in the decade 1866–1875, departed within that period as well. Between 1876 and 1885 the turnover was the same; 65 percent of those who arrived had also departed within a ten-year span.[38]

The family of glassblower Jean-Claude Peguignot offers a typical illustration of this pattern of migration. It was first listed in the Carmaux census for 1876. Peguignot and his wife were both born in the department of the Jura, and probably married there since their first three children were also born in the Jura. (These three, all sons, were listed as verriers in 1876.) Their fourth child was born in the Marne, their fifth in the department of Saône-et-Loire. The next child was born in the Haute-Marne, the next in the Loire, another in Saône-et-Loire, and the last in the Tarn at Carmaux. The oldest son, Hippolyte, came with the family to Carmaux, where he worked as a glassblower. He married the daughter of a miner in 1879 and then apparently left to work elsewhere for a time. His first two children were born in the department of the Nord, the other three after his return to Carmaux.[39]

Hippolyte Peguignot's moves away from and back to Carmaux are characteristic of many of his fellow glass-workers. Jean Cassier and his wife were born in the depart-ment of Nièvre. (Cassier's mother was born there as well.) Their first three children also were born in the Nièvre. Their next child was born in Saône-et-Loire in 1867. A year later, the family had apparently returned to the Nièvre, where Louis was born. In 1869 the family had moved again to the Loire; by 1871, they were in the Rhône. They went back to the Nièvre a second time in 1874, but shortly returned to the Loire, where their ninth and last child was born. In 1876 they arrived in Carmaux, but were gone by 1881.[40] Glassworker Jean-Louis Chaubard, the son of a carter, was born in Carmaux in 1841. He apparently emigrated to the Gard and returned, in 1866, with the family of Toussaint Rauzier. In 1868 he moved to Bordeaux, where his first son was born. By the time of the birth of his second son in 1870, Chaubard was back in Carmaux where, after yet another intermediate step, he finally settled in 1875.[41]

In a letter written in 1893, another glassworker described his travels. His account, one of the few provided by a glassworker, exemplifies the pattern which emerges from the civil records: "I have been a glassworker all my life . . . since the age of nine years. [I worked] at Rougemont from 1866 to 1875 when I went to Valur, then to Bordeaux. I returned to Rougemont in 1886 . . . [went] to Creil in 1887 and since the month of January, 1890, I have been at Bradville."[42]

Since their stay was short, glassworkers rarely bought property. Under Solages's administration they lived on the grounds of the château. After 1862, they rented lodgings in the streets surrounding the glass factory. All the censuses for Carmaux from 1856 to 1901 revealed the same geographic concentration of glassworkers. Although miners lived scattered throughout the commune, the names of almost all glassworkers could be found on two or three successive pages in the census book. The nature of their work dictated these living arrangements. They worked long and late hours, and in the winter a long walk would have been detrimental to the already weakened physique of the glass-blower. In addition, rotation of équipes and the system of replacements (by which a substitute was awakened to take the place of a worker who reported sick) were simplified by having all workers living near the shops.

The glassworkers' living arrangements, in turn, created a sense of themselves as a self-contained, separate community within the city. The glassworkers were isolated because they had no roots in the area and by their inability to speak the *patois*, the local dialect spoken by peasants and by the miners who constituted the bulk of Carmaux's population.[43]

The tremendous turnover in the glassworker population reinforced the social, economic, and geographic distinctions which separated glassworkers from other workmen in Carmaux. Glassworkers simply did not remain in Carmaux long enough to establish bonds with any but their own families and fellow-workers. Contacts within the craft apparently facilitated movement from town to town and region to region, and one's occupation as a glassworker earned one immediate acceptance in a community of glassworkers in any particular town. It is not surprising, given the specialized and segregated lives they led, that glassworkers identified themselves neither as townsmen nor as workingmen, but as members of a "corporation" of artisans whose prosperity and identity rested on the skills they possessed rather than on the town they lived in, or the particular establishment at which they worked, or their collective strength embodied in any formal organization. The corporation meant the craft or, more precisely, the body of craftsmen joined in an informal institution based on a network of kinship and mutual contacts which facilitated communication and informally perpetuated traditional standards of quality and terms of apprenticeship. As long as the blowing of bottles required difficult and highly specific skills, those who mastered them shared a common occupational and social experience. For the glassworkers of Carmaux it was an experience which for generations had isolated them from and established their superiority to all other workers in the town.

Glassworkers and Miners: A Contrast
3
_____

An isolated, changing community of strangers, the glass-workers were watched carefully by the police commis-sioners of Carmaux. Unlike the town's only other and much larger workforce, the miners, who constituted a stable peasant population, traditionally rooted to the soil, the glassworkers seemed a potential source of disturbance and disorder. They "do not share the moderation and wisdom of the miners," wrote one commissioner, "but their number is not great enough to cause fear of serious complications."[1]

Yet one searches the records in vain from 1752 to 1882: no "complications" serious or otherwise seem to have occurred. On the other hand, at least in the nineteenth century, Carmaux's miners were a frequent source of dis-turbance and even of disorder. If records of strikes and of arrests for participation in strikes are compared, there emerges a sharp contrast between the collective actions of the two groups. Carmaux's miners struck six times from 1855 to 1870 and some forty-nine of them were arrested in connection with these strikes. Glassworkers neither struck nor engaged in any other disorderly collective actions.[2]

The strike records of Carmaux's miners and glassworkers are typical of the national strike patterns of each trade before 1882. French miners held 106 strikes between 1830 and 1880, as compared with 9 by glassworkers. Whereas their record places miners high on the list of strike-prone trades, glassworkers are at the bottom of these lists. In addition, although miners' strikes erupted in most mining centers, strikes of glassworkers concentrated in two places: Lyon and Rive-de-Gier, large industrial centers with strong political traditions. Like Carmaux, the numerous other glassblowing centers of France never experienced any labor conflict.[3]

The explanation for the differences in strike activity between the trades has little to do with numbers, as the police commissioner suggested. It is true that glassworkers were few compared to miners. From 1862, when he opened the Verrerie Sainte Clothilde, until 1882 Rességuier employed a maximum of 250 men. The Société des Mines, on the other hand, increased its workforce from 1500 in 1856 to 2065 in 1883.[4] But although the relatively small number of glassworkers might account for the absence of "serious complications," it could hardly account for the fact that no actions of any sort occurred. Rather, the explanation for the differences in the activities of Carmaux's miners and glassworkers lies in their different histories in these years, in differences in the structure and organization of their work, and in the different patterns of their lives.

The histories of each trade were tied to the economic growth of France. French industrialization, however gradual in the first half of the nineteenth century, created

constantly increasing demands for coal. And mineowners
were under pressure to increase their output by making
work processes more efficient. Although wine was France's
second largest export and wine production an expanding
operation, traditional methods of bottle production were
apparently adequate to meet most demands. Some bottle
manufacturers tried to increase their labor forces by hiring
foreign-trained workers or by undercutting the souffleur's
control of his apprentices' promotions and they continued
expanding their operations. But, until 1879–80 (and then
only at the largest manufactories) the established organization of production was never altered, nor did machines
replace the glassblowers' skill.[5]

In Carmaux, the national trends could be observed in
miniature. Although Rességuier expanded the glassworks
by building new furnaces and additional workshops and
warehouses, he neither altered nor modified the traditional
organization of bottle production. In contrast, work at the
mines underwent a slow but important transformation
between 1850 and 1870. The Solages family business
became a corporation in 1853, and the paternalistic local
ownership was replaced by a board of directors in Paris
made up of men less accessible and less sympathetic to the
peasant-miners under their direction. In an attempt to
rationalize and increase output, the administrators of the
new Société des Mines de Carmaux modernized some of its
equipment, replacing men in certain jobs with horses or
machines, and, as noted above, they had a railway line built
through the city in 1864.[6] But above all, they sought to
make disciplined "professional" miners of their peasant
employees.

Living in the countryside adjacent to the mines, Carmaux's

miners had for generations labored in the pits only when they were not needed in the fields. In the 1850's they were characterized as: "undisciplined, lacking assiduity, with little professional competence, they give to the mine only a minimum of their time and even then they work as little as possible . . . only enough to obtain the supplementary amount necessary for their support, the essential part of which is assured by tilling the soil."[7] From 1850 to 1870, the company attempted to correct this situation and was met by resistance, usually in the form of a strike. In 1856, when the Director of the Mines, hoping to increase each miner's output, announced that piece wages would be substituted for daily wages, the miners struck and retained the hourly wage. Each time the working day was lengthened, the miners refused to work. Strikes in 1857, 1859, 1862, and 1869 were instrumental in preserving the eight-hour day.[8] In addition, a certain passive resistance to innovation accompanied the miners' strikes. Despite company threats to fire absent employees, frequent absences continued. Another aspect of the company's plan to make mining a full-time job was to force miners off the land. If they no longer owned property or lived in rural areas, it was argued, the miners would not interrupt their labors to plant or harvest their crops, and they would become completely dependent economically on mining. Thus in 1867 the Société des Mines began construction of a *cité ouvrière* of small houses and gardens which it hoped would lure a permanent mining population to Carmaux. The cité remained unfilled, however, until 1875, when the company made it a condition of employment that miners live within five kilometers of the pit at which they worked.[9]

After 1870, the company's policy began to succeed and the miners' resistance declined. Although the traditional eight-hour day remained in force, hours at the mines were reorganized to reduce the time miners could spend in the fields. Piece work wages were instituted successfully, miners began moving into Carmaux, discipline was enforced, and production and profits began to go up. In part, the company succeeded by virtue of its own persistence; but increasingly the Tarn's peasants had little choice. Mining offered better wages than did agriculture and, although one could continue to subsist on the land despite the agricultural crisis, the mines offered a positive opportunity for improvement. Once the triumph of the company was clearly established, no miners' strikes occurred for thirteen years. And, after 1883, when the miners formed a union, strikes were called on issues different from those in 1850–1870 when, as Rolande Trempé has concluded in her massive study: "what moved the miners of Carmaux was a desire to conserve their liberty to exercise a parallel agricultural activity. In fact, their behavior expressed a refusal to evolve, to adapt themselves to conditions . . . of industrial work."[10]

Thus a major reason for the different behaviors of Carmaux's miners and glassworkers stemmed from the fact that miners were experiencing changes in traditional practices and glassworkers were not. Certainly glassworkers elsewhere in France were not averse to striking, usually for reasons similar to those of the miners. Of the nine strikes they held from 1832 to 1879, seven were concerned with enforcing customary rules of apprenticeship or with opposing "new conditions of work." Only two sought a raise in wages (and these occurred in 1853–54, a year of severe economic hardship and high food prices).[11] Presumably, Carmaux's glassworkers would have struck had Rességuier introduced basic innovations.

Change itself was not, however, a necessary cause of

discontent. Measured in terms of wages, moreover, the changes experienced by Carmaux's peasant-miners represented an improvement over their former situation. Yet these same changes, by incorporating them into an occupational structure which deprived them of a former autonomy, made of the miners a more dissatisfied and potentially volatile workforce and increased their distance and sense of difference from the glassworkers.

For the most part, the men who worked at the mines of Carmaux from 1850 to 1880 did so increasingly out of necessity. Their distaste for mining was manifest in many ways: in frequent absences and in large-scale desertions for any other lucrative occupations, regularly for sowing and harvesting, and, in the late 1860's, to work on the railroad lines or to travel on them to cities. Mining represented a way of supplementing declining agricultural incomes in a period of continuing "crisis" in the Tarn. The agricultural crisis affected small landholders above all. In 1851, the Procurer Général of Toulouse wrote that "the misery of small proprietors is extreme; they are obliged to sell their goods at low prices, and often their properties as well."[12] A number of statistics reveal the continuation of this situation for the next decades. Between 1860 and 1880, the price of a hectare of land fell from 2000 to 1800 francs.[13] Migration from the area increased as peasants were forced to sell off their lands. (Only the urban centers in the Tarn, and Carmaux above all, experienced any influx in this period.)[14] Those peasants who did not permanently quit the countryside entered the mines. In the 70's and 80's, two-thirds of Carmaux's miners were sons of small property owners, the rest were sons of agricultural workers and rural laborers.[15] By 1882, most miners were described as landless, "having no resources but their work at the mines"—the reverse of the situation in 1850.[16]

As agricultural incomes continued to decline, wages paid at the mines increased, as did the miner's dependence on his wages for subsistence. From 1853 to 1882, average daily wages increased at a rate of 2.3 percent annually. The increase was more gradual from 1853 to 1868 (0.9 percent a year) and more rapid after 1868 (3.3 percent a year). At the same time, however, the cost of living increased more rapidly than wages, resulting in an overall decline in real wages between 1845 and 1882. Trempé calculates that the price of bread rose 13.26 percent (between 1845 and 1873) while potatoes rose some 70 percent and meat more than 50 percent.[17] As miners depended less and less on agriculture, monetary income became more and more important, for they had to purchase many more items, particularly food. A report on the economic situation of miners in 1882 contrasted the difference in life-style of the peasant-miner and the full-time miner. The differences noted capture the nature of the changes which began to be experienced decades earlier: "The worker-proprietor has the major portion of the provisions necessary for maintaining his household . . . a small salary is sufficient for him and he is easily satisfied with it. Because his work as a miner still permits him . . . to work on his small patrimony, which he cultivates and seeds according to the season. This category (of worker) makes no demands . . . because everything goes well, whereas the others will be pushed by necessity to make demands . . . [for they are] individuals who have no other resource but the product of their labor [in the mines]."[18] Thus, though comparatively higher nominal wages at the mines lured many peasants permanently away from agricultural pursuits, they were far from content with their new situation. In fact, miners were more sensitive than ever to fluctuations in their earnings, more anxious to protect wages from being lowered either absolutely or as a result of modifications such as piece wages, and more than ever aware of the insufficiency of what they earned. Their preoccupation with wages was manifest in every strike they held between 1855 and 1869, although wages themselves were not usually the precipitating causes of the strikes. In 1857, 1859, and 1860 Carmaux's miners demanded that wages not be lowered; in 1855, 1862, and 1869 they asked that wages be raised.

The position of glassworkers in Carmaux, on the other hand, made them less anxious about wages and less sensitive then the miners to small fluctuations either in daily wages or in the cost of living. At Carmaux, the glassworkers' real wages declined between 1862 and 1882, because, while prices rose, wages remained the same. Yet no demands were made nor actions undertaken to protect wages, for the glassworkers continued to enjoy a measure of comfort which other workers did not. And in Carmaux, when a glassworker compared his wages to what they had been at other glassworks, he knew his situation had improved absolutely. Rességuier paid his workers more than any other employer in France, and most glassworkers in Carmaux were comparing their wages not with those of earlier years in Carmaux, but with what they had received at Saint Etienne, Rive-de-Gier, or Givors. In the context of high rates of geographic mobility, a decline in local real wages had no impact on the glassworker's perceptions simply because he did not experience it. Thus, whereas wages were not a source of dissatisfaction for glassworkers, they were persistently central to the miners' concerns.

Their increasing dependence on their wages at the mines was but one indication of the loss of autonomy which becoming a miner entailed for the peasants of the Tarn. Mining never gave miners the control over their work which glassworkers enjoyed. The glassworker's skill created a finished perfect product. Without him, his employer would have no bottles to sell. Not only the quality and quantity but the very existence of wine bottles depended on the souffleur's ability to blow them. In addition, the glassworker's monopoly of skill meant that only he could train new craftsmen. By contrast, the miner's work involved the removal of a raw material from the earth. His abilities influenced only the rapidity, the safety, and ultimately the fact of its removal. The skills involved in mining were essentially manual and could be acquired rapidly and they could be taught not only by miners but by qualified supervisors and engineers. Although most supervisors were promoted from within the ranks of the miners, they were no longer considered workers, but, like the engineers, representatives of the company—agents imposing the company's will on its workers. No such division between supervision, technical knowledge, and manual skills existed at the glassworks. The souffleur combined the role of supervisor and workman. In the mines, technical knowledge belonged to the owners; in the glassworks it belonged to the workmen. Whereas the nature of their skills enabled glassworkers to control the conditions of their own work and employment, nothing in the miners' position gave them such control.

Nonetheless, as long as mining was a supplementary occupation, those who chose it had a certain autonomy. They could choose to work or not depending on need, or the weather, or the season, and they could quit if the work became burdensome or a supervisor too harsh. In this situation, the company appeared a neutral, if not benevolent employer dependent on the peasant-miner's willingness to serve it. As conditions changed after 1850, however, and miners increasingly depended on the company, they began to resent its exercise of total and often arbitrary authority. The resentment became increasingly bitter in the context of the company's drive to discipline its workers by giving supervisors the power to fine workers for latenesses and absences and also to fine them for more and less serious abuses. "We do not want a father to be fired because he has taken his son from the mines to have him learn a trade," the miners insisted in their list of demands in 1869, "nor should a son be fired because his father does not want to work."[19]

In addition, the supervisors and not the miners themselves were responsible for measuring the distance picked into the vein of coal each day. Since the miners' wages depended upon accurate measurements, they continually protested abuses and inaccurate measurements. Trempé records a series of attempts by the company to appease disgruntled workers:

May 30, 1861, the workers were invited to attend the measuring in order to avoid all errors of daily measurement by the supervisors; June 13 of the same year, after numerous complaints, a master-miner was specially charged with supervising the measuring by the supervisors, who in August received general instructions about keeping the records; May 17, 1864 the measurers in two pits were reminded of the order; September, 1872, the consulting engineer was obliged to specify that one of the essential points to observe in the conduct of the workers was to respect the rules of absolute justice . . . in measuring their work and regulating their wages.[20]

Not only wages but promotion to coveted higher paying positions depended upon the will of company representatives. Unlike glassmaking, in which the term of apprenticeship was established by tradition and in which the acquisition and perfection of certain skills meant recognition for a worker as a master of his craft, mining had no "organized or rational apprenticeship." A young man usually began working on the surface as a shale sorter. When he descended into the pits, it was first as a wagon puller. He then worked at increasingly difficult tasks and after several years might become a miner or *piqueur*, wielding the pick which loosened the coal from the earth. The decision about promotion was not made by those he worked with. Rather it was "a unilateral decision of the Société."[21]

A young miner's advancement depended as much (and often more) on the goodwill of his supervisor as on his professional abilities. This situation exacerbated the hostility of miners for their immediate supervisors especially, a hostility which was expressed above all in individual acts of defiance. Such acts occurred frequently enough to require regulation by the company. In 1860, for example, the Directors ruled that "the failure to execute orders . . . insults to overseers, master-miners, or other employees of the company will be punished by fines, suspension or firing, depending on the severity of the case."[22] The order did not eliminate the problem, however, and, for many years after 1860, the amount of fines and the number of days of suspension were increased annually.[23]

Except in these individual acts of disobedience or by hurling personal insults at their supervisors, miners had no means of expressing dissatisfaction with the organization of work at the mines. Acts of defiance, however, even if they did not bring dismissal, rarely brought any redress of grievances. The lack of any grievance procedure was explicitly exposed in one of the strike demands of 1869. "We demand a regular inquiry to air and to evaluate the grievances which we may have."[24] The absence of such regular inquiry and the continuing inability of the miners to express and resolve their discontents resulted in the perception of a common identity in opposition to their "oppressors" and in collective actions which attempted to create an authority of miners in opposition to the authority of the company. In June, 1859, for example, when the Director announced that the work days would be lengthened to ten hours, a group of wagon pushers left the pits together at the end of the usual seven-and one-half hours, forcing the company to concede. Again in 1862, 150 of the wagon pushers and loaders refused to enter the mines until the Director restored the eight-hour day.

The strike of 1869, which involved almost every category of miner was the culmination of these earlier efforts. In June, the miners demanded not only higher wages and the maintenance of the eight-hour day but the resignation of M. Chassignet, the hated Director of the Mines, as well as the firing of a number of supervisors. The administrators of the company saw the challenge for what it was and refused even to negotiate the issue of the director and supervisors. All of the difficulties created by the strike, wrote one administrator, "are less irreparable than would be the abandonment of our authority for ever." "The workers have no right to make such a demand."[25] A refrain of the strike song clearly expressed the miners' position: "To arms, let us rise up and rejoice: we vow to exterminate the tyrants of our shops."[26] The strike was clearly a means of relieving the miners of the "tyranny" imposed from above. When the company continued to refuse to fire Chassignet, the miners took matters into their own hands, invaded his house, and threatened his life if he did not immediately leave Carmaux. The authority of collective violence prevailed in the end over the power of the company. And a new director was quickly sent to replace the terrified Chassignet.

Although no continuing organization seems to have existed to call and lead strikes, a regular procedure did develop over the years. Strikes were generally announced on Saturday; the miners met on Sunday and elected committees to handle organization and negotiation; and on Monday, the strike began.[27] The strikes themselves built a sense of unity among the miners as well. In 1869, the solidarity created lasted for months. The miners continued to exercise their power even after they had returned to work. The administrators of the company described "a permanent complaint about all that involves the company."[28]

The events of February-March, 1870, well illustrate the situation. On February 22, twenty miners left a pit for a day to demand higher wages. On February 24, the miners at pit number two protested the rates for piece work by leaving their posts. On February 27, two piqueurs refused to accept the wages offered them. Followed by at least sixty other miners, they went off to complain to the engineer. During the conversation, the two threatened their superior, who then suspended them and ordered them out of his office. A large, angry group of miners gathered outside his office and was then dispersed. The next day, the piqueurs went out on strike. On March 12, fifty miners at another pit refused to descend into the mine until the Director promised repairs. On March 14, the Director's office was invaded by some fifty miners demanding the reinstatement of some workers who had been suspended for demanding higher pay. In the ensuing melee, two miners were arrested.[29]

Almost every week, another incident occurred, leading the administrative council of the mines to search for all possible means to "break, as soon as possible, the solidarity the workers invoke constantly, threatening that if one of them is fired, they will rise up en masse."[30] The use of "solidarity" to characterize the sentiments of the workers is significant. Usually the terms "coalition" or "conspiracy" were used in connection with unionlike activities. Those words implied a small group of agitators stirring up their fellow workers. Solidarity, however, denoted a wide diffusion of feeling, a sense of unity among most of the miners. For the miners, militant strike action created what the union would later institutionalize: a collective authority to force redress of grievances by their employer. In addition, it defined their relations among themselves in opposition to the company. It also provided a certain control over conditions of work that they did not have otherwise. In a sense, the strike provided for the miners what the structure of their craft provided the glassworkers.

At the glassworks, the souffleur was both skilled laborer and supervisor, and his interests and those of his apprentices were similar. Traditionally, the souffleur controlled hiring and firing and the pace and quality of work. He kept his own records of the number of bottles blown and supervised the payments to his apprentices. Promotion of these apprentices was also set by tradition and determined by the souffleur's judgment of a young man's ability to blow bottles. Unlike the miners, glassworkers were virtually assured of eventual accession to the pinnacle of the craft hierarchy. When grievances did exist they were usually resolved without hostility and without resort to strike. The statutes of the Chambre syndicale d' Aniche in 1882, give some insight into how grievances were handled in an earlier period. By 1882, the union performed what earlier, individual craftsmen had been able to do for themselves or for one another: "When a difference arises between an employer and a union member on a question of work or of wages, the union will take into hand the cause of its member. If it considers it just, it will try to obtain an amicable solution. If the affair has to be brought to court, the union funds will pay for the costs of a trial."[31] The differences were between individuals, the union (like the souffleur in a former period) merely provided moral and financial support. If the issue could not be settled "amicably," the case went to court. There was no question at all of collective protest.

Neither was there a sense of oppression expressed in the strikes of glassworkers that did occur. Rather than use the strike as a means of winning control they did not have, the glassworkers used it to protect the control they traditionally enjoyed. When a coalition of glassworkers was formed in Lyon in 1839 to "revive the rules for barring all apprentices but the sons of workers," officials feared that the old guild was being revived.[32] In 1847, 1859, and 1863, the same issue was at stake: protection of the privilege of glassworkers to determine who might enter their craft. And in 1854, 1877, and 1878, they struck to protest their employers' unilateral decisions to alter the customary "mode de travail."[33] Even when glassworkers did call strikes, they appear to have been immediate responses to an incursion of privilege or tradition, rather than the culmination of long-standing, unresolved grievances. The fact of skill and its associated privileges and traditions put the souffleur in a powerful position in relation to his employer. And the hierarchical structure of work gave an apprentice the protection of his souffleur as well as the assurance that he would not always be subordinate to him.

There was yet another means of expressing dissatisfaction traditionally open to glassworkers which did not exist for the miners of Carmaux. The craft had long been characterized by patterns of itinerancy and in the 1860's and 70's, the abundance of jobs created by the expanding bottle industry permitted the glassworkers tremendous geographic mobility. Even if he had no other means to express his discontent, a glassworker could always move on. Thus in 1859, when their employer refused to accede to the striking souffleurs' demand that he not hire a certain type of apprentice, they simply left the factory and found work elsewhere. The glassworkers' geographic mobility also minimized the effect of firing as a sanction of their employers. Whereas a fired miner was a man permanently barred from practising his trade, a fired glassworker was merely between jobs, a situation he often experienced by choice. Miners thus needed the protective authority of collective action, while glassworkers were protected individually by their skills and their ability to move.

Because of their rural attachments, migration was not really an option for Carmaux's miners. In fact, for many the choice of mining meant an explicit rejection of migration as a way of improving their situations. Eighty-five percent of the miners employed in Carmaux were recruited within twenty kilometers of the town between 1848 and

1914. In the 1850's through 70's more than half of them
owned houses. Most of the rest were share-croppers or part-
time agricultural laborers. Only a few had no landed
connections at all, since most miners were sons of peasants
even if they no longer worked the land themselves.[34]
Historic ties of friends and family, their ancestral roots in
the Tarn, kept miners in Carmaux and made their economic
dependence on the company total. Yet these associations
also had a unifying effect which permitted a certain spon-
taneity of action, which enabled strikes to take place,
endure, and sometimes succeed. Trempé puts it best:
Despite divergences of occupation and position within the
mines, "the miners appear to us linked by their common
geographic origin and thus by the nature of their former
[agricultural] activity . . . these former peasants knew the
same style of life, observed the same traditions and spoke
the same language: languedocien."[35] Common origins,
shared traditions, the familiarity of long family associations,
the continuity of personnel in the town and in the mine
created conditions which easily supported strikes. The
memory of earlier years could be preserved and transmitted,
and continuity of leadership assured. Thus, Jean-Baptiste
Calvignac always carried with him a recollection of the
strike of 1869, which he had witnessed at age seventeen.
His father had participated in it and had been among the
leaders of a partial strike in 1871. Calvignac became an
officer in the miner's union in 1883 and, eventually its
most outstanding leader. Calvignac's memory and his
father's experiences, like those of so many other miners
and their sons, created a tradition which nurtured activities
like strikes.[36] Ties of this sort, like informal meetings at
cafés, can never be completely documented. Even for care-

ful police informants, customary activities and familial conversations are not open to scrutiny. The repetition of strikes, the rapidity with which committees were created once a strike was declared, and the frequency of miners' strikes in Carmaux, however, lend support to the argument that "considerable stability of the working class at least within a given city . . . would seem to be a minimal necessity if mere complaints are to be translated effectively into class grievances and to inspire collective protest."[37]

The collective protest of Carmaux's miners in this period directly reflected their experiences. They attributed their oppression to the tyranny of their supervisors and to the more remote, less visible policies of the Société des Mines. The link between oppression and their employers was constant, since the miners remained always at Carmaux. And when they generalized about employers, the miners had only one experience which informed their generalizations. The glassworkers, on the other hand, experienced a number of different relationships with different employers and they tended to express their antagonisms against specific individuals; generalizations about all employers were more difficult to maintain. Their geographic stability in part enabled the miners to develop a collective identity in opposition to their employer, while the geographic mobility of the glassworkers perpetuated the sense each had of his individual identity in negotiating with different employers. Even if the glassworkers had had collective grievances in this period, it would have been difficult for them to act. Few glassworkers in Carmaux had been born there and most remained for only a brief number of years. Most rented lodgings; in fact only twenty-eight bought property from 1860 to 1890, and these were usually men who had been born in the vicinity of Carmaux.[38] Although they shared a strong craft identity, glassworkers had little chance to develop the personal connections outside their families which would have created and sustained strike efforts.[39]

Two populations of workmen lived side by side in Carmaux. Yet the fact that large numbers of them worked in capitalist enterprises did not give them a common class identity. Instead they were separated by profoundly different occupational experiences. These different experiences marked their behavior, leading miners to engage in strikes, while glassworkers did not. After 1880, the great differences between miners and glassworkers diminished in Carmaux as both groups experienced major occupational changes, but particularly as the elite position of glassworkers was undermined by the mechanization of their craft.

Mechanization

4

Changes in the Craft

"In entering the heart of the establishment and its workshops, I realized immediately that they had undergone a transformation so complete, and enlargements so considerable that there was no comparison I could establish between what existed when I last visited in 1865, and what exists today. The entire establishment, which at the beginning consisted of one furnace and occupied only a small area, now covers an area of more than three *hectares* . . . The principal buildings consist of vast halls, solidly constructed . . . providing the best technical conditions required by the glass industry."[1] So wrote M. de Planet, the inspector for the Exposition Décennale de l'Industrie à Toulouse, of the Verrerie Sainte Clothilde in his report of November, 1883. He estimated that Rességuier's improvements and the five additional furnaces diminished personnel costs since almost the same numbers of auxiliary workers could service six furnaces as one. His profit in 1883 on 10 million bottles was 310,000 francs. Planet concluded that with a new type of furnace Rességuier could do even better. The furnace he referred to was the Siemens gas furnace which was then in use at a few large glass houses. Although the Siemens furnace was available to French glass manufacturers as early as 1867, it was used primarily by window-glass makers who sought to maintain a competitive lead over the Belgian window-glass industry. It was not used in a bottle factory until 1878, when M. Richarme installed it in his plant at Rive-de-Gier (Loire).[2] Richarme was at the forefront of the French bottle industry's drive to consolidate and to introduce new technology which would reduce production costs. (The drive was spurred in part by English competition in the export market. About one-quarter of the bottles produced in France were exported in 1878. In addition, the growth of several large bottle manufacturers within the country spurred domestic competition as well.)[3] Richarme had been buying out small glass houses in neighboring departments for several years, as had another of his competitors in the region, the Compagnie Générale des Verriers de la Loire et du Rhône. Shortly after Richarme installed the Siemens furnace, the Compagnie Générale and another Lyonnais bottle manufacturer converted as well. The greatest asset of the new furnace was that it reduced fuel costs and permitted continuous production. Richarme and his associates could sell bottles more cheaply than smaller manufacturers who did not have the capital to build new furnaces and who could not afford to suspend production while they were being built.

Rességuier, however, was in a position to compete with manufacturers like Richarme, and he clearly intended to establish his hegemony in the region of the Tarn. He not only built his factory on the railway line, but he also had

obtained preferential shipping rates from the railroad
company. (His drive for success even led him to dishonesty:
he was found guilty in 1890 of having stolen a patented
process for making molds from a rival company.)[4] In 1884
Rességuier took M. Planet's advice; he transformed his
individual proprietorship into a corporation and introduced
the Siemens furnace into his factory. The incorporation of
the business appears to have had little effect other than to
increase the capital available for mechanical improvements.
Rességuier and his son-in-law continued to maintain exclusive control over the direction of the glassworks. The
changes in techniques of production, however, had an
enormous impact.

Under the new system the old *fours à pots* were replaced
by *fours à gaz* (or *fours à bassin*). In the fours à pots,
crucibles full of the raw materials were placed in the furnace at noon. At midnight, the melted glass was ready for
the blowers. This system divided the work day into two
parts. For twelve hours the furnace was heated, bottles
blown the preceding day were annealed, and crucibles were
prepared and filled. In the next twelve hours, bottles were
blown. With fours à gaz, the melting process was continuous.
Flames of gas (derived from coal) controlled the fusion of
primary materials which were injected mechanically into
the furnace and emerged as molten glass at various openings.
With this system, the day was divided into three eight-hour
shifts, and bottles were blown during every shift.[5]

The eight-hour shifts permitted by the fours à gaz
changed the glassworker's style of life as well as the organization of his work. Though the work day was shortened,
the pace of work quickened. A team produced many more
bottles in an hour than previously. In fact, the reporter for

the Exposition Universelle de Paris in 1878 had warned of the "serious" economic consequences of the new system in which "each shift can produce triple the number [of bottles] ordinarily obtained."[6] In addition, a kind of leveling took place with the introduction of eight-hour shifts. No longer was a special time of day accorded the glassworker. Despite the fact that the heat of the new furnace was much more intense than before, he was expected to work in the afternoon as well as at night. Like the miner, his shift was rotated on a daily or weekly basis. The new schedule also doubled the workforce at the Verrerie Sainte Clothilde. Reports to the Prefect of the Tarn from the Mayor of Carmaux, and presumably based on Rességuier's records, indicate a tremendous increase in glassworkers employed after 1885. Between 1876 and 1884 the number of employees varied from 200 to 265, while by 1885 the figure had nearly doubled to 447.[7] The same increase is confirmed by the censuses. The largest increase in those glassworkers enumerated came between 1886 and 1891—the years following the introduction of the fours à gaz.[8]

The doubling of Rességuier's workforce represented a trend in the bottle industry which had as its effect increasing unemployment for skilled and experienced souffleurs. As the large plants expanded, producing larger quantities of cheap bottles, smaller glassworks were driven out of business. Their craftsmen could not easily find work at the large plants, however, for they found themselves competing with less skilled younger men. The pool of available workmen increased far more rapidly in the 1880's than did the number of available jobs since in addition to the new furnaces, which changed working conditions for everyone,

Table 12. Number of Employees at the Verrerie Sainte Clothilde, 1871 and 1876–1887

Year	Men[a]	Women	Children
1871	200	20	60
1876	240	20	60
1877	250	20	50
1878	250	20	50
1879	250	20	50
1880	250	20	50
1881	260	20	30
1882	265	21	30
1883	200	50	50
1884	250	40	80
1885	447	101	58
1886	430	98	57
1887	450	200	150

Source: A.D. Tarn, X M 3 3.
[a]This includes men of all categories, auxiliaries as well as glassblowers. However, the greater percentage increase in the number of women employed indicates that women were being used to perform certain auxiliary tasks once done by men. Other reports indicate that the largest increase in male personnel was among the *verriers*, since the same number of *similaires* could assist even double or triple the number of verriers.

Table 13. Number of Glassworkers Arriving in Carmaux, by Decade, 1856–1895

Years	Number	Increase (magnitude)
1856–1865	47	—
1866–1875	105	2.2
1876–1885	234	2.2
1886–1895	465	2.0

Source: Family reconstitution.

other mechanical devices were introduced which required less skill of the master craftsman. Until the introduction of the *moule fermé fixe* and the *moule fermé tournant*—stationary and revolving closed molds—the shape of each bottle depended on the souffleur's lung power, on the regularity with which he turned the tube through which he blew, and on his judgment.[9] Unlike the open molds, closed molds guaranteed a standard form for each bottle, and the moules tournants eliminated the possibility of defects in the shape and consistency of the glass. The new molds enabled skilled souffleurs to increase their output.

And, by simplifying the skills required, they opened the position of souffleur to young men with less training and ability than was formerly demanded and (to a much lesser extent) to older men, whose failing strength or ill-health once had forced them to leave the craft or accept lesser positions within it.[10]

The influx of young men is strikingly demonstrated in the graphs of the age structure of glassworkers in each of the censuses from 1866 to 1896. Whereas until 1886, the largest increases occurred in the age ranges twenty-five to thirty-nine, by 1891, the most dramatic expansion had occurred in the youngest age range (ten to nineteen). In 1876, too, there had been a noticeable increase in glassworkers aged fifteen to nineteen, but it was matched by an increase in those aged twenty-five to twenty-nine. This was clearly a result of expansion. Rességuier had opened two new furnaces in 1875 and recruited both older souffleurs and younger apprentices.[11] In contrast, in 1891, the much smaller increase in any other age category but the youngest indicates not only expansion but a drop in the age of souffleurs.

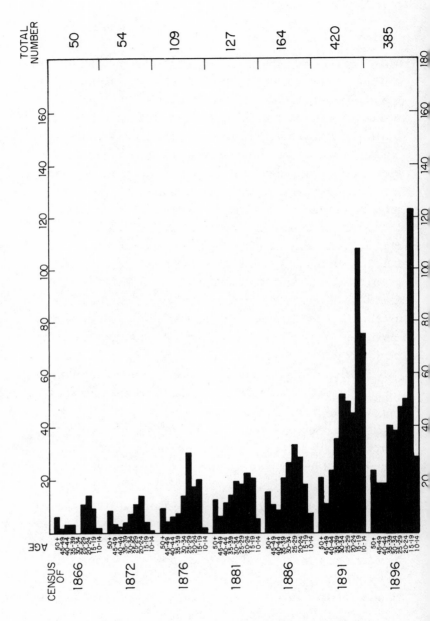

2. Age structure of glassworkers in Carmaux, five-year periods, 1866–1896.
Source: Censuses, 1866–1896.

Not only were younger glassworkers being hired at the Verrerie Sainte Clothilde, they were increasingly local young men whose fathers were not members of the craft. In the decade 1876 to 1885, only 9 percent of glassworkers married were born in the Tarn. Yet, in the period 1886–1895, 18 percent of those married were born in the Tarn, and by 1896–1905, 61 percent of the glassworkers married in Carmaux listed the Tarn as their birthplace. (See Table B, appendix). The increase in locally born glassworkers corresponded to a decrease in representation of sons of glassworkers. Whereas 40 percent of all glassworkers married in the decade 1876–1885 were sons of glassworkers, in 1886–1895, this figure dropped to 21 percent and then to 13 percent in 1896–1905. (See Table A, appendix.) In the censuses the contrast was even more pronounced. While 55 percent of those glassworkers aged ten to nineteen were sons of glassworkers in 1876, only 17 percent of the same age group were sons of glassworkers in 1891. (See Table C, appendix.)

The simultaneous increase in demand for workers and the downgrading of the skills required of them began to change the relationships between accomplished craftsmen and their apprentices. The system of production by équipes consisting of a master, two apprentices, and bottle carrier, and supported by a host of skilled and unskilled auxiliary personnel was the same as it always had been, but the training of apprentices changed considerably. The union statutes of 1892 specified the duration of each stage of apprenticeship as one to two years.[12] Thus, beginning as a gamin at age twelve or fourteen, a young man would be ready to assume the position of souffleur by age seventeen or eighteen. Once, an apprenticeship of fifteen years had been

79

required; now it was at most five years. In fact, the level of skill required of a glassblower was so much lower that young men were being hired as souffleurs who had not even completed an abbreviated training as a grand garçon. Furthermore, hiring and promotion were being taken out of the hands of souffleurs by employers, who needed no mastery themselves to judge a young man's ability to blow bottles. The influx of these unqualified young men led a Congress of the National Federation of Glassworkers to resolve in 1893 that workers under twenty could not replace souffleurs.[13] The need for the ruling seems to support the evidence in the censuses and to indicate that men under twenty were being permitted to blow bottles. One glassworker, his whole tone conveying a certain exaggeration, even referred to instances of fifteen-year-old souffleurs and grands garçons of twelve.[14] The statement was made in the heat of a debate over trade-union tactics and was intended to score polemical points. Nonetheless it indicates that the influx of less skilled young men—children in the eyes of older, highly skilled souffleurs—was considered a real and serious threat to the traditional age and skill hierarchy of the glassworks. If the pressure for advancement of grands garçons and gamins were not stopped, warned a glassworker from the department of the Nord, then skill would no longer protect established workers who did not meet all the "exigencies" of their employers. The leveling implications were clear: "What is done in the mines, will be done at the glassworks."[15]

But the most far-reaching and indeed the most disturbing effect of the new technology was overproduction of bottles compounded by a drop in demand. As the Verrerie Sainte Clothilde increased production to 33,000 bottles a day the demand for bottles was suddenly and dramatically reduced by phylloxera, the disease which attacked grapevines and crippled wine production in the Midi. In 1883, the Tarn had 49,386 hectares of vine under cultivation, but in 1888 there were only 27,901 hectares. The harvest in 1883 was 1,150,255 hectolitres, five years later it had dropped to one-tenth that amount or 100,047 hectolitres.[16] Everywhere the situation was the same. The French grape harvest declined from 46,165,006 hectolitres in 1883 to 24,031,771 in 1889. Recovery did not begin until 1893 and even then yields remained considerably lower than in 1883.[17]

The mechanization of production had already reduced the value of a glassworker's labor; overproduction worsened the situation. As a result the wages of glassworkers dropped, an event unprecedented in the memory of most of these craftsmen. At the Verrerie Sainte Clothilde the souffleur's average daily wage dropped from twelve francs in 1885 to nine in 1886; that of grands garçons fell from five francs to three francs fifty. Similarly, the average daily wage of French glassworkers fell from five francs twenty-seven in

Table 14. Average Daily Wages at the Verrerie Sainte Clothilde, Selected Years, 1876–1887 (Francs, Centimes)

Year	Workers over 21	Workers aged 15–20
1876	12.00	5.00
1882	12.00	5.00
1885	12.00	5.00
1886	9.00	3.50
1887	9.00	3.50

Source: A.D. Tarn, X M 3 3.

1882 to four francs fifty in 1891–1893.[18] And although the cost of living decreased between 1880 and 1890, wages fell at a faster rate. Nor could a decrease in living costs offset the psychological impact of receiving considerably less money for a day's work.[19]

But perhaps most troubling of all, the power to change the situation lay outside the glassworker's control. His traditional responses for dealing with grievances no longer worked. The skill he possessed gave him no bargaining advantage with his employer and if he quit his job there was no guarantee he would find another one. For the first time in the history of the craft the power of the employer did not depend on his highly skilled employees. Rather the possession of capital enabled Rességuier and others like him to introduce mechanical substitutes for human skill. In 1878 an observer had warned of the effects of mechanization in the glass industry: "If in many industries the substitution of mechanical for manual labor offers important advantages because . . . it decreases a man's fatigue, we do not think it will have the same effect on the absolutely

Table 15. Average Daily Wages of Glassworkers (All Departments, except the Seine), Selected Years, 1882–1893

Year	Francs, centimes
1882	5.27
1885	5.37
1888	5.35
1891	4.75
1892–1893	4.00–4.50

Source: *Statistique générale de la France*, 1885 and 1891–1893.

special work of the glass industry, and we fear that in depriving glassworkers of difficult tasks we will destroy their skill as well as the artistic talents of which glassworkers have the right to be proud."[20] Not only the loss of pride but the loss of power affected glassworkers in the 1880's. The options available to them were limited by decisions their employers had made and over which they had no control. Yet glassworkers' responses to the new situation involved both an accommodation to it and an attempt by new means to recapture control of their craft. They sought to protect their jobs by reversing earlier patterns of itinerancy and to reassert their power and their pride by forming trade unions.

Settling in Carmaux

With a bottle surplus throughout France, a glassworker's economic security began to depend upon keeping the job he held. Moving to a new place entailed the risk of unemployment; a glassworker might have to travel long and far to find a factory with openings. Claudius Saintoyen, and his father, both glassblowers, arrived in Carmaux in 1893 hoping to find employment. When none was available they wrote to several places and finally received word of openings at Chalons-sur-Saône, 270 miles away. "Unfortunately," the police report on them concluded, "having no resources, they were obliged to go there on foot."[21] Another glassworker reported an even worse aspect of the situation: "When, for whatever reason, [a glassworker] is forced to move from his factory, he goes elsewhere with a provisional title, or even worse, he is demoted to an inferior position as a grand garçon or *cueilleur de verre*. In the present state of things, this happens three-quarters of the time."[22]

The alternative chosen by glassworkers was to stay where they were. All the data indicate a marked drop in geographical mobility after 1885. Although 65 percent of those arriving in the period 1876–1885 departed within the same decade, only 42 percent arrived and departed during the years 1886 to 1895. Put in other terms, persistence rates for glassworkers in Carmaux rose from 34 percent in 1876–1885 to 57 percent in 1886–1895. (See Table D, appendix.) The high rate of geographic mobility in the period 1876–1885, and its dramatic drop in the succeeding ten years is highlighted and confirmed when rates of new arrivals to Carmaux, as measured by family reconstitution, are contrasted with the rates of increase in the personnel at the Verrerie Sainte Clothilde as officially reported by Rességuier. Although two times as many newcomer families arrived in Carmaux during 1876–1885 as had come in the preceding decade, the work force did not grow substantially at all. In the next decade, however, the increase in new arrivals paralleled the increase in the glassworkers employed at the glassworks—in 1886–1895 there are slightly fewer than two times as many new arrivals and slightly fewer than double the number of employees as in 1876–1885. (See Tables 12 and 13.) The discrepancy between arrivals and the number employed in 1876 to 1885 indicates a tremendous turnover in the glassworker population in these years and confirms the departure figure in the table based on family reconstitution data. Further, the fact that *both* the number of new arrivals and the number of glassworkers employed doubled in 1886 to 1895 indicates that those glassworkers who came to Carmaux in this decade remained in the town.[23] The increased stability of Carmaux's glassworker population was in part the result of a change in recruitment; many more natives of the Tarn than ever before found jobs at the Verrerie Sainte Clothilde after 1885. In addition, however, formerly mobile glassworkers had begun to settle in Carmaux, as demonstrated by the experience of the Peguignots.

As it typified glassworker mobility in an earlier period, the Peguignot family also best illustrates the settling process after 1885. Having worked in at least seven different departments over the course of twenty years, Jean Claude Peguignot, who arrived in 1876, apparently decided to settle in Carmaux. His oldest son, however, left shortly after his marriage in 1879 and sought work in the department of the Nord. Perhaps because his family was still there, Hippolyte (born 1854) returned to Carmaux in 1886 where he remained for the rest of his life. His two sons, both of whom became glassworkers, never left the city of their birth. One was married in Carmaux in 1907, the other in 1911. The second Peguignot son (born 1856) followed his older brother Hippolyte's pattern. After his marriage in 1881, he departed for Saône-et-Loire, but he, too, returned to Carmaux ten years later. His sons, both glassblowers, settled and married in Carmaux. A younger Peguignot, François Clément (born 1871), fifteen years younger than his older brothers, began work at the Verrerie Sainte Clothilde in 1886. He never left the town. He was married in Carmaux in 1905, all his children were born there, and there, too, he died. The first generation of Peguignots moved on the average of once every three years. The oldest sons of the next generation began to repeat their father's pattern. They apparently found it unsatisfactory and began to settle in the late 1880's. The third generation of the family evinced a decided absence of geographic mobility.[24]

Similarly, glassworker Nicolas Gand, before arriving in Carmaux in 1881, had moved his family at least three times over the preceding thirty years. Although his two oldest sons had married during the family's sojourn in the Dordogne, both followed their father and younger brother to Carmaux, where they all settled. Edouard (born in 1850) died in Carmaux in 1908. All of Louis's sons became glassworkers, married, and began their families in Carmaux. Paul (born in 1861) married a local miner's daughter. His children married and died in Carmaux or neighboring Albi.[25]

In addition to settling in Carmaux, Paul Gand acquired some land, like an increasing number of glassworkers in the last years of the nineteenth century. In fact, in the ten years from 1890 to 1900, four times as many glassworkers bought land for the first time as had in the preceding decade. (The glassworker population in 1890 and 1900 was about double that of 1880 to 1890.) Although the number of glassworkers owning property in Carmaux was always relatively small (at most the glassworkers who were landholders represented no more than 8 percent of the glassworking population), the increase in those who did purchase land after 1890 is further evidence of a tendency to settle in the town. (It also reflects the increasingly local, noncraft origins of glassworkers, who, like their fathers, wanted to maintain traditional family ties to the land.)

The end of geographic mobility and its concomitant local recruitment meant that glassworkers were less isolated from other workers in Carmaux. Certain of their demographic patterns, however, continued to differentiate them from others in the town. Death especially more frequently struck young glassworkers and their infants, even though their situation had improved for the most part over earlier years. Although the miners' average age at death dropped to fifty-four years and eleven months by 1903–1912, the glassworkers' average age at death was thirty-five years and six months in 1896–1905.[26] Neither measurements of average household size nor of marital fertility indicate any significant changes in the glassworkers' practices, but the data on fertility are too scattered to be conclusive. Even if certain of their life experiences were different, however, settling in Carmaux nonetheless brought glassworkers in contact with other workers in the town and it also meant that more lasting ties could be established among glassworkers themselves, providing them the basis for formal organization in a specific collective identity as employees of Rességuier and as residents of the city.

Unionization

As they adjusted their individual lives to the effects of the new technology, glassworkers joined collectively to deal with the problems created by mechanization. In 1890, 300 glassworkers at the Verrerie Sainte Clothilde signed the first membership list of the Chambre syndicale des verriers de Carmaux.[27] A year later, with a membership of 430, Carmaux's union affiliated with the national Fédération du Verre, which had held its founding congress at Lyon in 1890.[28]

Carmaux's union was formed by men who, for the most part, were socialists when they arrived in the town. In particular, the glassworkers from Montluçon, Michel Aucouturier, Jean (Marien) Baudot, and Maximilien

Charpentier have been cited by historians as the prime cause of glassworker activity in the 1890's.[29] The Montluçonnais had been fired during a strike in 1888 and shortly afterwards recruited to Carmaux by Rességuier. Montluçon was early a center of influence for the ideas of the French Marxist leader Jules Guesde, and the Guesdist leader Jean Dormoy had a large following among the city's metal workers and glassworkers.[30]

The group from Montluçon, with about ten or twelve others, notably the brothers, Phillippe and Louis Renoux, Emile Renard, and Marius Rauzier stand out distinctly within the glassworker community. Their names appear again and again on police lists of "dangerous . . . revolutionaries," in court records of arrests for participation in strikes, on lists of socialists contending local elections, on unions and strike committees, committees of miners and glassworkers preparing May Day demonstrations, and in newspaper accounts. When Rességuier absolutely refused to rehire some twenty-two of his workers after the strike of 1895, almost all fourteen of those we have designated "leaders" were among them.[31] Police agents may have confused ideologies, calling a man anarchist or socialist somewhat indiscriminately, but invariably their characterization of him as a "leader" corresponded to his role in union and political activities.[32]

The leaders were visible not only as a political group. They tended to form a kind of social "inner circle" within the glassworker community. Their names appear together as frequently on one another's marriage, death, and birth acts as they do on police lists. The social connections among glassworker leaders followed from family ties as well as repeated political contacts. Whether the links pre-

dated or followed their appearance in the town, however,
the leaders' closest associates at work were frequently
family members. Bonds of comradeship were reinforced
by family ties. Louis Renoux married Marien Baudot's
niece in 1894. Louis's sister Marie wed Martin Gidel,
secretary of the glassworkers' union in 1894.[33] At Renoux's
wedding Maximilien Charpentier, Baudot, and Michel
Aucouturier served as witnesses. Charpentier's sister married
militant unionist Louis Charrier.[34] And Michel Michon was
a cousin of Charpentier. Four families provided the central
network among the leadership: Baudot, Gervier, Gidel, and
Renoux.

The role of these leaders in Carmaux seems at first to
support an explanation frequently given about the development of socialist ideas among French workers. Historians
of French socialism, like the socialists themselves, argued
that ideologically developed leaders played a determining
role in the formation of working-class consciousness and in
the organization of working-class institutions. Carmaux
glassworker Marien Baudot understood his own role in this
way. Describing the union as a "school" in which workers
learned to "combat their oppression," he stressed the role
of teachers. "Nothing can prevent the idea of socialism
from spreading among the masses . . . But those who, like
us, are the first to see the light must continue, more than
ever, to lead the way."[35] Baudot himself illustrates the
limitations of his own interpretation, which, if it is accurate in one sense, nonetheless distorts the history of the
French labor movement. For the emphasis on ideology
and institutions underplays and obscures the experiences
and actions of French workers. Undoubtedly Baudot and
his comrades' ability as leaders rested on the fact that they

were socialists. They had a clear sense of direction, organizational models, and, above all, a language with which to articulate and conceptualize the problems faced by glassworkers. But their ideology alone does not explain why the leaders defined issues as they did, why their organizations took specific forms, and why they succeeded in securing so large a following among their fellow workers. In fact, the success of the leaders was less a product of their ideology than of their ability to offer a concrete program for solving glassworkers' problems. This program came not from their ideological orientation but from their own experiences as glassworkers. Marien Baudot and his comrades were socialists, but they were also glassworkers, and if we examine the content of their socialism and the goals of their union we find them preoccupied with the same problem as their followers: the preservation of their status and economic position as skilled craftsmen.

In one sense, the union represented an acceptance of new conditions: it helped to institutionalize the end of geographic mobility. The *syndicat* often was conceived of as a fortress within whose walls worked a stable population of glassblowers. The union would protect its members not only from wage cuts and other such maneuvers of their employer but also by preventing "strangers" (from other glassworks in France) from entering an establishment. The speeches and articles of glassworker leaders developed a new theme: the longing of the glassworker to live in his home town. Marien Baudot, one of the founders of Carmaux's union, spoke of the desire of all men for a small house and garden, of their identification with the "small glassworks, now vanished," in the towns of their birth.[36] Philippe Claussé of Toulouse offered an elaborate plan to the national congress in 1891, to stop the "avalanche of young workers." He insisted that apprentices be promoted to souffleurs only as existing places were vacated and that "nominations [for employment] be made exclusively in the locality where the trainee had completed his apprenticeship."[37] Even the question of wages was related to the end of geographic mobility. The general strike of 1891 demanded a unified wage schedule for glassworkers in all of France. With a single wage, some argued, workers would have little incentive to move to glassworks which paid more and would remain settled in one place. In 1895 Maximilien Charpentier, another leader of Carmaux's union, offered a plan by which the union could limit the number of apprentices trained and promoted. "In the future," he urged, "an apprentice must not be allowed to take a position unless it is permanently open—that is unless its occupant is dead."[38] Significantly, a vacancy created by the departure of a souffleur for other parts was not even mentioned.

But if the glassworkers were willing to reverse traditional patterns of itinerancy, they nonetheless refused to accept the destruction of glassblowing as a skilled trade. The goal was stated plainly by a delegate to the national congress in 1892: "It follows, citizens, from all we have heard and understood . . . that overproduction, aided by a surplus of workers, will lead to the complete destruction of glassworkers; who in several years have become human machines. If we do not react, our craft will fall."[39]

The union was formed in an attempt to save the craft—not, however, by blocking Rességuier from introducing new techniques nor by pressuring him to maintain old production procedures. The union did constitute a powerful opponent to Rességuier on such issues as wages and recruitment; but initially this was not its most significant function. More importantly, the union served as a substitute for the old organization of work at the glassworks. As mechanization leveled the hierarchy of skill, the union sought to maintain it by providing its members (and indeed all workers at the Verrerie Sainte Clothilde) with the structure that was once inherent in the craft.

As expected, the most skilled glassworkers, the souffleurs, reacted most sharply to the changes in their occupation. Not only their jobs but the high status and pay that their positions represented were in jeopardy. In addition, their place at the head of an équipe and their role as teachers of the craft made them the natural leaders of their fellow-workers. Indeed, the membership list of the Chambre syndicale des verriers in 1890 included almost every souffleur at the Verrerie Sainte Clothilde. Other glassworkers joined the union too, for preservation of the craft hierarchy meant guaranteed promotions for them. The grands garçons had almost as great a stake as the souffleurs, for their wages and their futures as high-paid craftsmen also were adversely affected by mechanization. Yet their role in the union was less marked, in part because they were younger and used to following their masters' lead and also because their jobs were not as immediately threatened. Grands garçons and gamins attended meetings and joined strikes, but the leadership of both the local union and national federation consisted entirely of souffleurs.

Carmaux's leaders present a particularly striking example. Like most glassworkers in Carmaux in 1890, all but three of the leaders arrived after 1885. All fourteen of them were souffleurs. (See Table 16.) Their average age in 1890 was twenty-six; the oldest was thirty-seven. The group was not unusually young, although the absence of older men made it unlike the general population of glassworkers.[40] Carmaux's earlier militants (who would have been older than the leaders of the 1890's) may have shared the fate of Camille Pradel who was six years old when his glassworker father brought the family from Rive-de-Gier (Loire) to Carmaux in 1866. As soon as he was old enough, Camille, like his brothers, began training as a glassworker. In his early twenties, Pradel began organizing his fellow workers. He lost his job at the Verrerie Sainte Clothilde, probably after the strike in 1882, and went to Cagnac "where, with new ardor, he engaged in the struggle against the tyrant Boucher," owner of a large glass factory. Pradel soon found himself again without work and he left France to rally glassworkers in Spain. Driven from Spain, Pradel finally returned to his family in Carmaux. Sick, and an old man at thirty-four, he died on October 26, 1894.[41]

If potential union leaders like Pradel were driven from Carmaux, it might be expected that men like them, driven from other glassworks, would assume leadership when they arrived at the Verrerie Sainte Clothilde. But this was only partly the case in the 1890's. The life of Emile Renard, the oldest of the militants, was probably similar to Pradel's. Renard arrived in Carmaux in 1894 at the age of thirty-seven, having worked in at least two departments. His entry into the town was heralded by a police report which noted that he was a "very dangerous revolutionary socialist."[42] Like Renard, the five glassworkers from Montluçon, were "political" figures when they came to the Verrerie Sainte Clothilde. Yet most of them had been born in Montluçon and had never left until they were forced out. Of course, they had been long steeped in a socialist tradition.[43] But despite their socialism, the glassworkers from Montluçon, and most of their fellow militants in Carmaux, were not leaders of long experience like Pradel and Renard.

Their youth and the dates of their arrival in Carmaux indicate an additional if not a different sort of explanation for their militancy. All had been apprenticed before the introduction of fours à gaz. Most must have expected to follow the career patterns of their fathers, if not to improve on them. Half of the leadership group were sons of glassworkers. (This is significantly larger than the glassworker population as a whole in Carmaux with some 20 percent sons of glassworkers in 1890.) Two more were sons of blacksmiths who had probably been employed at a glass factory. They began training when the position of a souffleur was still an enviable one among workers. Just as they attained mastery of their craft, however, machines began to make mastery unnecessary. The leaders were unlike their predecessors (and fathers) who had enjoyed a relatively privileged status for a number of years and who might, even with fours à gaz, maintain that status a bit longer before retiring. And they were unlike the increasing proportion of glassworkers for whom entry into even a modified craft represented great improvement over their fathers' economic situation. Though mechanization began by 1876 at Rive-de-Gier and Givors, only one of the leaders came from that region. Most came from factories which introduced fours à gaz at about the same time Rességuier did, in the mid-1880's. Thus, although vaguely threatened by reports of new developments, they must have expected that the position of souffleur would remain a special one, at the pinnacle of the craft. The coincidence of their completion

Table 16. Glassworker Leaders in Carmaux, 1890–1895

Leaders	Age in 1890	Birth date	Birth place	Father's occupation	Date of arrival in Carmaux	Previous residence	Number of moves before arrival
Michel Aucouturier	26	1863	Montluçon (Allier)	Glassworker	1889	Montluçon	0
Jean (Marien) Baudot	22	1868	Montluçon	Blacksmith[a]	1890	Montluçon	1
Louis Belin	24	1866	Montluçon	Unknown	1891	Montluçon	0
Jean Boyanique	21	1869	Béat (Nièvre)	Unknown	1892	Unknown	—
Maximilien Charpentier	31	1859	Melun (Cher)	Glassworker	1890	Montluçon	2
Louis Charrier	30	1860	Vernaison (Rhône)	Glassworker	1876	Rhône	0
Martin Gidel	20	1870	(Creuse)	Glassworker	1890	(Aisne)	1
Michel Michon	24	1866	Montluçon	Blacksmith[a]	1886	Montluçon	0
Celestin Nicholas	22	1868	(Herault)	Unknown	1891	(Herault)	0
Marius Rauzier	35	1855	Alais (Gard)	Glassworker	1866	Alais	0
Emile Renard	37	1853	(Dordogne)	Farmer	1891	(Vendée	2
Louis Renoux	20	1870	St. Léger-des-Vignes (Nièvre)	Glassworker	1886	(Nièvre)	0
Philippe Renoux	31	1859	(Cher)	Glassworker	1886	(Nièvre)	1
Auguste Sallès	32	1858	St. Hilaire (Gard)	Farmer	1881	(Gard)	0

Source: Family reconstitution.
[a]May have worked in glassworks.

of apprenticeship and of the devaluation of the status of the souffleur must have heightened their preoccupation with the problems of glassworkers. A newly promoted souffleur in his early twenties usually could marry with a certain security about the future. He might have to move several times, but the skill he had spent some eight or ten years acquiring, would ensure employment at a comparatively high wage. In 1885, however, a newly promoted souffleur was faced with the fact that the skill he had spent so many years learning was rapidly becoming outmoded. Economic security, and even continued employment, no longer were guaranteed.

Moreover the insecurity of many of the leaders was heightened by the fact that they were forced to move to Carmaux. This move affected them more than other glassworkers; many had never left the place of their birth until they came to Carmaux. Of the five from Montluçon, only Charpentier had not been born there. Marien Baudot had departed briefly when, at age eight, he accompanied his brothers to a glassworks in Cormontreuil (Marne), where he served as a *porteur* for several years. But Baudot soon returned to his birthplace and completed his apprenticeship there.[44] Like the Montluçonnais, the remainder of the leadership moved little, if at all, before they came to Carmaux. Of the fourteen, two arrived in the city as very young men. The record of one other is unknown. Of the remaining eleven, only five had worked in towns other than their birthplace. Even these five moved at most twice and usually only once before coming to Carmaux.

Whether forced to move for political reasons or out of economic necessity, moving when they did must have intensified the insecurity of these young souffleurs. They were accustomed to a relatively stable existence in a familiar setting. Philippe Renoux, who was ten when his father brought the family to St. Léger-des-Vignes (Nièvre), and Louis, who was born at St. Léger, received their apprenticeship training at a single glassworks. Not only did they expect to enjoy the same position their father held, they probably expected to hold it at the same glassworks. Their lives must have been doubly disrupted when neither expectation fully materialized.[45] Carmaux's leaders would have identified, more than many glassworkers, with Marien Baudot's description of the nostalgia of those who were "natives of all those small glassworks which have disappeared." "One always has a bit of preference for his native country, sometimes he has parents, friends and family there, or perhaps a small piece of land whose value increases when an industry begins or expands . . . one treasures the hope of spending his old age there."[46] This statement could only have come from someone of Baudot's experience and not from the vast majority of glassworkers who had moved as often as once every three or four years, whose families and friends were dispersed in glass centers throughout France, and who rarely stayed anywhere long enough to acquire either "preference" for a particular place or "a small piece of land."

Baudot rejected the possibility of returning to earlier conditions. In effect, however, he urged glassworkers to settle anew where they were. The guarantee of their jobs no longer lay in the existence of numerous small glass factories, but in collective action by glassworkers—in union. For the leaders settling involved the creation of working-class institutions, rather than the purchase of land. This outlook was the product of contact with and acceptance of socialist ideas and it equipped them with a program of action to offer their fellow workers. As newcomers to Carmaux they immediately undertook the organization of a union. In addition, however, leadership in the union gave these young souffleurs a defined position among glass-workers. As heads of committees, as representatives to Rességuier, they attained the sense of control over working conditions ordinarily felt by the master of an équipe.

At Carmaux, the souffleurs used their positions at the pinnacle of the hierarchy of skill to establish the union and they used the union in an attempt to maintain the control of all aspects of their work which had once accompanied their mastery of the skill of bottle blowing. The union was organized according to équipes, with a union member responsible for each *place* at every furnace during every eight-hour shift. The souffleur, as head of his équipe, traditionally had a say in the hiring and firing, the punishment and promotion of his apprentices. Since most souffleurs belonged to the union, they often forced their assistants to join by threatening to dismiss them if they refused. The statutes of the Chambre syndicale des verriers, like the rules of the medieval guild (and in much the same language—a language strikingly absent from the miners' union statutes) regulated the terms of apprenticeship as well as the internal operation of the union.[47] If a gamin or grand garçon violated the rules of the workshop by blowing a bottle, for example, then the union fired him or increased his term as an apprentice. In 1894, a souffleur reported that his porteur, one Bousquet, had been caught blowing a bottle. Bousquet's promotion to gamin was delayed for six months, and all members of the union agreed to enforce the punishment.[48] After completing his one-and-one-half-

year term as a gamin, a young man paid a specified sum to
the union before becoming a grand garçon. He paid an
additional fee when he graduated to the position of souffleur. If a glassworker failed to pay this fee, his union dues,
or to attend a meeting to which he had been summoned,
either he was fired, had his apprenticeship term increased,
or was refused work by his own and every other souffleur
in the glassworks. One gamin whose promotion was in
question clearly defined the alternatives when he reported
that his "father preferred to withdraw [him] from the glassworks rather than pay" the union.[49]

As the union punished erring or disobedient apprentices,
so it protected those who followed the rules. When the
employer overlooked a deserving gamin who had fulfilled
his training requirements, his souffleur and the union intervened to insure his promotion. In some cases, the power of
the union overturned a punitive action of the administration. When Elie Cadrieux, a grand garçon, was suspended
for eight days by Rességuier, his souffleur refused to take
on any other grand garçon and continued to allow Cadrieux
to work.[50]

The strength of their union organization enabled the
souffleurs to control some conditions of work as well as of
apprenticeship. In 1894, the union considered a request
from Rességuier to determine which furnace ought to be
used to produce a special type of bottle. The union determined the rotation system for the four mort and turned
down petitions by several members asking that they be
allowed to work elsewhere during their month of enforced
vacation. In accord with the notion of the union as a
fortress, the Chambre syndicale des verriers de Carmaux
notified all glassworkers (by advertising in the organ of the

Fédération du Verre, *Le Reveil des Verriers*) that those seeking work must apply simultaneously to the union and the employer.[51] In 1893, glassworkers in search of jobs were sent away by Rességuier, in compliance with the union's demands that no strangers be hired.[52]

Yet, although they achieved a measure of control at Carmaux, the souffleurs could not overcome the problems of overproduction and lowered wages. From 1890 to 1895 they considered a number of solutions, all of which, while attempting to retain the craft structure of bottlemaking, indicated that, in fact, it virtually had been destroyed. In the past, sons of glassblowers had enjoyed a certain priority within the trade. Most strikes of glassworkers which occurred before 1880 sought to protect the privilege "of the blood." Sons of souffleurs at the Verrerie Royale de Solages occupied special positions assisting their fathers until a place opened for them, and, under Rességuier, too, sons of glassworkers followed their fathers at the Verrerie Sainte Clothilde. But, by the 1890's, the idea that a father's skill constituted his son's legacy had been dropped. When delegates to the Congress of Fourmies in 1892 proposed that, as in the past, glassblowing be restricted to sons of glassworkers, they did so not because they believed in the glassblower's family's privileged status but because they felt it might be as convenient and as arbitrary a means as any other to break the influx of personnel.[53] The suggestion was defeated on two grounds. Ideologically, it introduced an element of superiority into the craft—one which separated the glassworker from his fellow workers. Despite their struggle to retain the glassblower's position and power as an artisan, many members of the Federation considered themselves socialists. The notion of special craft privileges was seen as an illusion, a device used by employers to appease their dissatisfied employees. But if the proposal was ideologically unacceptable, it was equally unfeasible for practical reasons. Restricting glassmaking to sons of souffleurs solved no problems either, for if all the sons of a glassworker had the right to enter the craft, the danger of an oversupply still existed. (On the other hand, if not enough sons chose to follow their fathers, the glass factories might be seriously understaffed.)[54]

Even more important, however, sons of glassworkers had to be prevented from competing with their fathers. Like other young apprentices, the glassworkers' sons were mastering the trade at an earlier age than had their fathers. When a young man became a souffleur, he came of age at work, and socially as well. With a souffleur's wages he could leave home, marry, and raise a family, thereby depriving his parents of his income, an income that became increasingly necessary as glassworkers' salaries declined. As younger and younger men became souffleurs they both hurt their families economically by cutting off additional funds sooner than in the past and they competed with their fathers for a job, thereby intensifying the threat of unemployment to the older man. For these reasons the souffleurs of the 1890's were not as interested in providing for their sons' futures within the craft as they were in keeping their own jobs, and the Federation resolved that apprenticeship be regulated for sons of glassworkers just as it was for everyone else.[55]

The solution most universally espoused from 1890 to 1895 involved limiting the numbers of available souffleurs by "regulation of apprenticeship." The phrase was on the agenda of every congress the Federation held in those years, and it headed at least one article in most issues of *Le Reveil des Verriers*. The phrase was a curious one. The notion of apprenticeship itself implied a certain regulation. It denoted a process of education in which length of training and standards of skill were set by the master craftsman and were accepted and adhered to by a young man as a condition of his learning the trade. Control of admission, selection, and promotion, even of the speed with which a pupil acquired his training, belonged to the accomplished artisan, whose mastery of skill permitted him control of the craft. The fact that an inherently regulated system needed "regulation," the redundancy of the notion of "regulation of apprenticeship" indicated how great a change had occurred. The numerous plans offered to achieve "regulation" acknowledged what the phrase implied: the end of the glassworker's traditional craft relationships.

At the same time most resolutions adopted to "regulate apprenticeship" attempted to reassert the form, if not the substance of older practices. These resolutions included limiting the age at which a young man could begin his apprenticeship and setting twenty as the minimum age for becoming a souffleur. At the Congress of Lyons in 1891, the Carmaux delegates moved that no gamins be admitted to a factory under fourteen years of age. Urging that all children be twelve before being allowed to work in any capacity, the representatives of the union at Rive-de-Gier combined horror for the fate of their children with an even more emphatic dread for their own future. "If . . . the masters are not prevented from snatching [young] children from their families . . . the craft will be destroyed. We will no longer be men capable of earning our living and we will face the triple alternative of poverty, suicide, or theft."[56]

This statement indicated that control of admission to the craft had been appropriated by employers, referred to as "masters" by the glassworkers. Once the term "master" had referred to the master craftsman and was used interchangeably with souffleur. Now, however, the term referred to the employer, whose ownership of the factory gave him a mastery, which had nothing whatever to do with skill. The artisans referred to themselves solely as souffleurs. The use of this functional term, which merely described what they did, denoted the loss of their mastery. The statement also represented the souffleurs' attempt to reassert a degree of control over the training process by setting age limits. Their actions, however, demanded only indirect control. For age limits were guidelines set for the employer, and there was rarely a demand that he completely relinquish his right to hire his own personnel.

Since tests for skill were increasingly somewhat arbitrary, and since with the new machines most young men could easily master the requisite skills, the Federation also attempted to regulate apprenticeship by lengthening the number of years of earlier stages of training. In 1892, for example, four years of preparatory work was suggested for young men entering a glass factory. After two years of carrying bottles or holding the molds, and another two years gathering or cleaning the molten glass, a young man might become a gamin or grand garçon, depending on the skill he had acquired.[57] Neither job, of course, really needed two years of practice. Rather than having the term of apprenticeship fit the requirements of the craft, however, the glassworkers used the old stages of training to deal with the new problem of numbers—a problem created by the downgrading of all skills involved in bottlemaking. By lengthening only the early stages of training (rather than every stage), the glassworkers acknowledged, if only tacitly, that the crucial skills of the souffleur could be acquired relatively quickly by gamins and grands garçons. The point was to delay for several years the initiation into the craft of the youngest and least able members of the hierarchy and thus to relieve the competitive pressure from grands garçons on the souffleurs. But if he began at age twelve, a boy would be sixteen when he began as a gamin. And, if he were quick, he would still be ready to be a souffleur at only eighteen or nineteen. This proposal, then, did not solve the most difficult problem facing the souffleur, that of the grand garçon.

The ability required of a grand garçon and of a souffleur had become almost indistinguishable. Often one man performed both tasks at a single glassworks, serving as a souffleur on one shift and as a grand garçon on another. Logically, then, one of the major factors in the control of apprenticeship involved the position of the grand garcon. When the glassworkers attacked the problem, however, they did not try to enforce a longer term of training. Instead, they attempted to make the position of the grand garçon a permanent one. The delegates from Carmaux suggested in 1892 that "all our efforts ought to be made to obtain . . . an increase (in pay) for the grands garçons."[58] If his remuneration were higher, added a representative of Megecoste, the grand garçon "could establish and raise a family [and] he would no longer consider his position as a transitory means for becoming a souffleur."[59] Increasing the status and pay of the grand garçon and making the post a permanent one meant the end of the apprenticeship system. In effect, it implemented a division of labor in place of the hierarchy of skill. At the same time, however, the intent of the resolution was to prevent less skilled workers from displacing established souffleurs. Initially, the glassworkers defined their right to control entry into the craft as a function of their skill. The power of the union, in this definition, lay in its grouping together of the most skilled workers in the shop, in its ability to coordinate their actions. The souffleurs assumed that by collectively refusing to transfer their skills, they might win their demands for higher pay and more regulated conditions. This assumption was a general one held not only in Carmaux but in the Fédération du Verre as well. In his summation to the second congress of the Federation in 1891, Philippe Claussé defined the "principal question" of the meetings as "the discontinuation of training apprentices." He saw it as "the surest and most efficacious means . . . to ameliorate our situation, because without pupils we will no longer have to fear this avalanche of young workers seeking our positions." By carefully regulating admission to the craft "we destroy the evil at its root . . ." and end "the decadence we are suffering."[60]

Claussé's argument was based upon the traditional assumption that the souffleurs he addressed could correct the situation by withholding their skills. They, and not their employers, this argument held, were true masters of the craft because of their ability to blow bottles. And by uniting and jealously guarding their mastery, the souffleurs might win their demands. In fact, many individual unions did seriously attempt to limit the number of apprentices admitted to their factories by refusing to "teach our craft." The names of those who violated their union's resolutions

were published in *Le Reveil des Verriers* and all other
unions were urged to prevent the hiring of these "traitors"
at any glass factory in France.[61]

Yet as the souffleurs pledged themselves to greater efforts
to limit apprentices, young men nonetheless continued to
be hired and trained by employers; as they resolved year
after year to limit production, stocks of bottles grew
steadily in storage rooms and warehouses and even when
they achieved a degree of control, as in Carmaux, it was at
the cost of continual struggle with their employer. By 1895,
few souffleurs relied on skill as a weapon in the struggle to
protect their jobs. "We must prevent apprentices from
having the capability to replace us," insisted Maximilien
Charpentier, the delegate from Carmaux, and "in the
future, an apprentice must not be allowed to take a position unless it is permanently open—that is unless [its
occupant] is dead." By "prevent" and "not be allowed,"
Charpentier meant through the force of union pressure. He
did not advocate the refusal to teach apprentices as a
solution in itself. For the employer could always find someone to teach the few skills required, or he could teach them
himself.[62]

What is important in Charpentier's argument in 1895 is
that, unlike Claussé in 1891, he located the power to
implement these demands not in the special skill of the
souffleur but in the strength of the Federation, in its ability
to mobilize glassworkers against their employers. What had
begun as a reassertion of the power of the souffleur became
an insistence on the power of the organization itself. Only
the political or economic force which the union represented, and *not* the collective skill of its members, could
ensure their future and protect their jobs.

Yet, this new definition of the union contained an unresolvable contradiction. At first, in 1891, collective skill had been depicted as the means for protecting the job and the economic position of the souffleur. Later Charpentier emphasized the union itself—its numbers and actions, its very existence rather than the skill of its members—as the means for protecting the souffleur. The goal was the same, yet the change in definition of the means indicated that the goal itself had become unattainable. If their skills were no longer needed, no organization could secure the souffleurs' jobs. Even a strong union ultimately could not triumph over the combined force of a powerful employer and economic circumstances which had all but destroyed the craft of glass bottle blowing. In 1890, however, this contradiction was not yet apparent, and glassworkers rallied to the union. Mechanization ultimately did destroy the craft of glass bottlemaking, but first it transformed the collective actions of Carmaux's glassworkers and the politics of the city as well.

Socialism

5

In 1882 a police report had found Carmaux's miners "animated by good sentiments . . . [They] are not concerned with politics, but exclusively with the interests of their trade." Similarly, although glassworkers were strangers and therefore not to be trusted, they were not reported to be involved in political activity. In general the report found that Carmaux's workers supported their government, they were "sincerely Republican; sure of themselves they go to the polls on election day without hesitation."[1] By 1893, however, the police lists of "dangerous revolutionaries and anarchists" in Carmaux consisted entirely of the names of glassworker and miner union leaders. This categorization of the union leadership may have been indiscriminate. Indeed, it was often hysterical. Yet it conveyed a change in the perception of union activity by police agents that corresponded to the increasingly political definition the unions gave to their own position. In Carmaux in the 1890's the unions led political action. Simply the fact of union membership had come to imply a political position; and most of Carmaux's workers were union members. The town councillors were all militant trade unionists in 1892, and the Mayor, Jean-Baptiste Calvignac, was the founder and secretary of the miners' union.

Although Calvignac belonged to no party, he, like most other workers in Carmaux at the time, described himself as a socialist. Some other of the union leaders did adhere to the politics of the Marxist Jules Guesde, but neither their policies nor those of most of Carmaux's workers can be categorized in terms of any particular doctrine or school.[2] Instead, the socialist politics of Carmaux can best be designated by what one historian has termed "labor socialism": "an empirical movement with a practical, non-doctrinaire and even anti-intellectual theory." Its roots lay in the experiences of workers in conflict with their employers and in their disillusionment with the labor policies of the Republican national government.[3] Calvignac described his own evolution exactly in these terms. "In 1884, the word socialist was almost unknown to me, I was content to be simply a Republican." But, by 1889, disillusionment forced him to change his views. "[I]f the workers' hopes are disappointed, they will turn either to reaction or to revolution . . . As for me, I will never be a reactionary republican."[4]

The socialism of Carmaux's workers included both trade-union activity and electoral politics. In the same year that they sent Jean Jaurès to Parliament they overwhelmingly endorsed the "immediate general strike" as the ultimate weapon of the social revolution. At the time that Fernand Pelloutier, theorist of revolutionary syndicalism, renounced Jules Guesde's Parti Ouvrier Français because of its insistence on the seizure of the political apparatus of the state, the miners and glassworkers of Carmaux endorsed both the general strike and socialist politics. The nationally advertised disputes of intellectual leaders seem to have had little relevance to the experience of Carmaux's workers. They felt no need to choose between strikes and elections. More important was the agreement on the need for concerted working-class action.

But what was the source of the agreement? When Rességuier and Solages asked themselves what had happened to disturb the calm of their enterprises and of their city, they usually blamed a handful of leaders of "bad faith." These men, slaves to "party spirit" had somehow lured their comrades into acts of insubordination. Yet even the Director of the Mines noted that leaders had been around for many years.[5] A socialist workers' circle had formed in 1882; then some glassworkers had attempted a brief strike; some miners struck and formed a union in 1883. What distinguished 1890 from earlier years was that the leaders now had followers, that their appeals met with widespread and overwhelming response, and that miners and glassworkers had a great deal in common whereas before they had not. Indeed, the emergence of socialism in Carmaux after 1890 can only be understood in the context of the fact that miners and glassworkers had come to share a many faceted identity stemming from similar experiences at work, within their unions and as residents of Carmaux. Socialism was not the product of the inevitable evolution of worker consciousness; rather it emerged from particular needs at a particular moment in time. That is why socialism took hold when it did in Carmaux, but also why its political triumph was so short-lived.

Solidarity

The formation of a glassworkers' union in Carmaux
paralleled the emergence of a reorganized and strengthened
miners' union. "For a year," the Director of the Mines
reported in 1892, "the peace of the shop has been profoundly disturbed. The socialist theories which for many
years were confined to a small group of the faithful, suddenly burst forth toward the end of 1890. The miners'
union, which had languished in the midst of internecine
quarrels, was reorganized. At the end of 1891 a majority of
workers had joined it and at that time began the campaign
of demands."[6]

The sudden success of the miner leaders stemmed from
changes the Director himself had overseen at the mines. As
glassworkers faced the problems brought by new machines
and overproduction, the miners of Carmaux confronted a
crisis of their own. A greater division of labor had accompanied the rationalization of production at the mines.
Tasks were more differentiated and hierarchically arranged
than before, but promotions remained the arbitrary pre-
rogative of supervisors. Accession to the coveted position
of *piqueur* was never certain, nor were the steps clearly
defined for an aspiring young miner. In 1890–91, the
situation was exacerbated when, as part of an expansion
program, the company hired large numbers of young men
in low-skill positions (as wagon rollers and aides). In a short
time it became clear that, for most, these jobs were to be
permanent, rather than the first step to higher-skilled,
better-paying places. For older miners the influx of young
men lessened the chances for advancement, and for the newcomers, upward mobility was blocked from the start.[7]

These conditions were particularly disappointing for the young men who were miners in 1890. Most were sons of miners following their father's occupations. Their fathers had been peasants for whom becoming miners (however difficult the experience) ultimately meant greater material security. Although for the sons mining did not provide the mobility it had for their fathers, they nonetheless looked upon it as a trade within which one could at least increase one's wages with age. In the circumstances of 1890–91, however, even this was not necessarily guaranteed. The plight of the miners' son, as described in 1901, began ten years before:

Oh, yes, gentlemen, the son of a miner is necessarily a miner and still remains one, not as you think for love of the trade, but necessarily, indispensably, by fate. What else can the son of a miner be if not a miner himself? Isn't he obliged, from his tenderest years to help his father build a house? . . . And . . . as soon as possible, the son of the miner, to add as much as possible to the [income] of the family, descends into the mines and once he has entered how do you think he can leave? What other trade can he learn? What possibility exists for freeing himself from the tutelage which weighs on him like fate? None; That is why the son of the miner becomes a miner as his son will become one one day.[8]

The tone of the young men of the 1890's was not as despairing as it would be a decade later. Instead, they joined the union, demanding that the Société des Mines regulate its production procedures, increase wages with length of service (regardless of tasks performed), and give preferential treatment to sons of miners. The average age of the members of the syndicat des ouvriers mineurs de

Carmaux fell from thirty-five in 1883–84 to nineteen in 1891–92, indicating that young miners particularly were dissatisfied with conditions at the mines.[9]

Although their specific situations differed, miners and glassworkers simultaneously confronted crises involving wages, job security, and opportunities for mobility. Whereas miners sought ways of guaranteeing pay increases, the glassworkers attempted to prevent wages from falling. Young miners particularly looked for upward mobility, the most skilled glassworkers wanted to keep from moving down. The younger men in both cases found their expectations of advancement disappointed; the older men wanted to protect themselves from being displaced by younger workers. The similar nature of their problems provided common ground for miners and glassworkers. They were able to understand one another's grievances since they experienced similar ones themselves. In the perception of these shared experiences they found an identity as workers which transcended particularistic notions of exclusive corporations or specific trades. "We are no more privileged than metal workers, miners [or] building workers," wrote a glassworker in 1893, "and our lives are much shorter."[10] And the miners' union opened its banquet of July 14, 1891, with a resolution beginning, "we, proletarians."[11]

The rhetoric of socialism was provided by the leaders, who for some years had been attempting to organize their fellow workers. But the concept gained meaning as miners and glassworkers sought solutions to their problems by joining unions. The Chambre syndicale des verriers and the Syndicat des ouvriers mineurs embodied the differences of the trades they represented. All miners, regardless of position, seniority, or skill, were grouped together in the union, which sought to "contribute to the moral and material progress of miners as well as to the legitimate satisfaction of their wishes and needs . . . to study the amelioration of their trade and to defend the individual interests of each of its members."[12] In contrast, the glassworkers' union gathered only skilled workers. Auxiliaries in the factory were relegated to a union of their own. And although the stated goals of amelioration of conditions and material improvement were the same, the forms of the two unions differed considerably. The miners' union statutes governed only the operation of the union, while the rules of work and of the union were intertwined in the statutes the glassworkers adopted. Only after several years did the glassworkers abandon their reliance on skill and arrive at the notion the miners had begun with: "The spirit of union and of solidarity . . . will be our force."[13]

Nevertheless, the fact of belonging to a union was more important than whatever differences characterized the two organizations. A union was a group of workers acting to win concessions from their employer. And the fact that two groups of different types of workers were opposing two different employers did not lessen the similarity of the experience. In fact, the ties between the employers were made explicit in 1890 when the Marquis de Solages, controlling owner of the mines, joined the Administrative Council of the glassworks. In addition, the institutions themselves created formal bonds by supporting one another's activities and jointly sponsoring meetings and demonstrations. During the glassworkers' strike of 1891, the miners' union sent donations to the strike fund. On May Day, 1891, miners and glassworkers participated together in a demonstration, and glassworker leader Michel

Aucouturier promised his union's support for the miners' campaign for the eight-hour day. "Your comrades, the glassworkers, who already have eight hours, have stopped work with you to show our solidarity."[14] During the miners' strike the following year, the glassworkers reciprocated their comrades' earlier financial assistance and they were among the crowds of miners who harassed police and invaded the Director's house.[15] The unions also jointly sponsored a number of clubs which grouped miners and glassworkers together for the study of social and economic questions.[16] And the miner and glassworker unions together sponsored candidates for the Municipal Council of Carmaux.

The unions' turn to electoral politics stemmed, in part, from their leaders' socialist convictions. The seizure of the state, some argued, could only follow the capture of the city hall.[17] Yet at Carmaux electoral politics followed naturally from union activities since the workers' employers also controlled the politics of the town. Though Rességuier was nominally a Republican and Solages a Legitimist, their interests were joined on most municipal issues. Throughout the 1870's and 1880's, administrators of the glass factory and at least one mining engineer served on Carmaux's Municipal Council, as well as on all juries and administrative bodies. But if they ran the town through assistants, the owners of the mines and glassworks represented their interests themselves in the Chamber of Deputies. Since 1876 Baron Reille, the powerful president of the Board of Directors of the mines of Carmaux, and the father-in-law of the Marquis de Solages, had been elected to the Chamber from the Tarn. Reille was also tied to the national organization of coal producers as one of the

founders of the Comité des Forges as well as a member of
the Comité des Houillères. Reille ran and was elected in the
second electoral district (Castres), which did not include
Carmaux. Nonetheless, he controlled politics throughout
the department and in 1889 was instrumental in securing
Solages's victory in Albi and Jean Jaurès' defeat in
Carmaux. (Jaurès had been elected as a Republican in 1885
and it was his influence especially among the miners and
glassworkers of Carmaux that the conservatives Reille and
Solages sought to defeat.)[18] In 1889 Reille and Solages
used the pressure of wages and fear on their workers,
threatening that Jaurès' victory would mean unemployment in the mines. They also used persuasion. "In recent
days," Jaurès reported, "workers who had always been
kept out of the great château, have been invited in; there
have been celebrations, a warm welcome, beer and tobacco,
a new familiarity."[19] When Solages joined the administrative council of the glassworks, Jaurès maintained that
Solages acted "not for industrial, but for political reasons,"[20] hoping thereby to secure the votes of the glassworkers as he did those of the miners. The employers thus
taught their workers the connections between their work
and politics, making it clear that to win a measure of
economic control meant also wresting political control
from their employers. For this reason politics became a
facet of union activity. And socialism expressed very clearly
the opposition of workers' interests to those of their
employers.

A Working-Class Community

Carmaux's two major unions were not only trade organizations involved in politics. They were the organizing institu-

tions of working-class life in the town. The social cohesion provided by the miners' and glassworkers' unions rested in part on the fact that by 1890 both groups of workers had begun to settle in Carmaux.[21]

Although miners had always been recruited locally, they were for the most part a rural population until 1890, when over 90 percent had moved to Carmaux or to one of two contiguous communes, Blaye or Saint Benoît. Life in the city brought with it problems not directly related to a man's work. For one, the miners had to buy more of their food. In addition, they could not rely on forests as a free source of fuel, but had to buy coal to heat their homes (there was never enough coal in the company's free allowance). And although housing might be more comfortable, it was much more expensive and more difficult to find, especially in the 1890's when large numbers of people were settling in the town. Whereas, in the country one was isolated from one's neighbors, in Carmaux, the density of population made one always aware of others. Thus appearance and style became more important, and, although the cost of living did not rise in the early 90's, it seemed to for Carmaux's miners. Rolande Trempé argues convincingly that this was a result of additional consumer needs created in an urban milieu. A city miner needed more clothing, food, and better household furnishings than his rural predecessor. In fact, by 1914, the item of greatest increase in a miner's budget after food, was clothing.[22] The press of other people and the impossibility of individual efforts to secure them made basic services like water supply, sewerage, and transportation more vital. Health and education also became matters of collective concern, because medical services and the staffing of schools were inadequate and were also monopolized by the employers.

These issues were increasingly important to glassworkers as well as to miners in 1890. Although glassworkers had long been city dwellers, they rarely before had been permanent residents. Their style of life did not change as drastically as the miners' did, but continued dwelling in one town sensitized them to changes in the cost of living and to the need for basic services. They could not go elsewhere if the city became intolerable because the security of their jobs now depended on their settling in Carmaux. This fact gave them another identity to share with the miners—they were all not only workers but Carmausins. For this reason, as much as for their leaders' ideological considerations, they sought to influence and win control of the politics of the city.

The stability of Carmaux's worker population also made greater continuity of organization possible. Twelve glassworkers had been listed among the twenty-six founding members of the socialist party-inspired Cercle des Travilleurs in 1882. Only six of them still lived in Carmaux in 1890.[23] Those who founded the union in 1890, on the other hand, remained in Carmaux (or, after 1895, in Albi) for at least the next twenty years. In addition, a more stable workforce at the factory gave the union greater organizing power. If fines and suspension could not coerce a reluctant glassworker into joining the union, the social pressure of the tightly knit, union-oriented community might make him change his mind. Similarly, canvassing for votes was facilitated if one knew all the names on the electoral list. And increasingly, if he refused to support the union and vote for the worker lists in elections, a glassworker found himself an outsider not only at the factory but among the entire laboring population of Carmaux.

Continuity of personnel within the city cemented the ties between miners and glassworkers, as well as among glassworkers themselves. They not only supported one another's union activity but met regularly on market days and in cafés. And although most glassworkers still lived in the two streets adjacent to the Verrerie Sainte Clothilde, the presence in the town of the same people, year after year, enabled them to break the barriers of language, geographic isolation, and itinerancy. Although miners' wives often worked after 1890 and wives of glassworkers rarely did, the women shared the problem of higher food prices and, undoubtedly, they spoke to one another of their difficulties when they met in shops, at the market, or on the street, their familiarity warmed by the fact that their husbands thought of one another as comrades. Social relationships were cemented further by the fact that families of miners and glassworkers were joined by marriage. And many more friendships were reflected in an increase in the number of miners appearing as witnesses at glass-worker weddings, as members of glassworker households in census listings, and as the godparents of glassworkers' children.

Social relationships, like union relationships (and largely as a result of them), were strongly influenced by politics. In fact, the personal and the political were no longer distinct realms in a worker's life. As membership in the union implied a political stance it also began to define (though less completely) a style of personal behavior. Strikes, meetings, and elections were natural occasions for political discussions, but marriages, baptisms, and funerals usually were not. Yet in the 1890's, these purely personal events became occasions for political manifestations, as the movement for civil marriages and burials grew. Indeed the refusal to accept the church's blessing was seen by some as the beginning of a peculiarly working-class practice. Events which were conventionally limited to family and friends became moments for the gathering of an entire class. In fact the anticlerical movement was led by the union leadership and even the terms defining it were borrowed from the union: "We are engaged in a strike against the priests."[24] The church embodied "the spirit of political reaction and religious fanaticism" and those who opposed it were involved in "revolt and emancipation" from "superstition and servitude."[25] Anticlericalism, it was argued, sought in the personal realm what union activity did in the economic, a workers's "freedom and the freedom of his children."[26]

As early as 1882, the statutes of Carmaux's socialist-led Cercle des Travailleurs stipulated that "at the death of a member a general convocation will be held and . . . members have a duty to attend the burial no matter what kind it is, but particularly if it is a civil burial."[27] The movement for civil funerals grew in the 1890's and, although the actual practice seems to have been limited to the most militant union leaders, hundreds and often thousands of Carmaux's workers attended them. In April, 1891, 600 Carmausins followed the coffin of the three-month-old daughter of Michel Aucouturier[28] and, a year later, more than 4000 workers heard Jules Guesde's oration at the civil burial of socialist Auguste Boyer.[29] Despite prohibitions by local authorities, red flags appeared at these ceremonies and speeches usually ended with the assemblage shouting "Vive la Révolution." Miners and glassworkers together accompanied the deceased to his grave. Glassworker leaders Marius Rauzier and Martin Gidel delivered the eulogy for the former miner Gaudin in 1891,[30] and Jean-Baptiste Calvignac, miner-mayor of Carmaux, led the cortège of glassworker Hippolyte Delrieu in 1892.[31] The speeches at the funerals invariably referred to the deceased as a "martyr" snatched from his loved ones by Rességuier or Solages. Children were described as victims of their parents' poverty, adults as victims of the glassworks or the mine. Personal loss and suffering were translated into political terms. Each death was, in effect, a murder which must be avenged by a continuing struggle against "capitalism" and by the final triumph of "the social revolution."

Perhaps because the wishes of the dead were always honored, more civil funerals occurred than marriages or baptisms. In addition, living persons incurred continuing harassment from local authorities, whereas the dead, once buried, were allowed to rest. When glassworker Nicolas Célestin and his bride arrived at the town hall of Blaye for their civil wedding ceremony, a frocked priest appeared before the couple. Upon questioning he turned out to be the assistant mayor who, disapproving of Célestin's intention to refuse sanctification of his marriage, intended to remind him of his obligation to the church. And when Marie Brunet was married to a glassworker in a civil ceremony in 1894, her mother was expelled from the Société de Sainte Thérèse, a woman's church group.[32]

Most of the opposition to the civil movement however, came less from church and city officials than from the wives of glassworkers and miners. Women constituted a major obstacle to the spread of purely civil practices, preferring traditional religious ceremonies for the major events of their lives. Speeches and articles in *La Voix des*

Travailleurs constantly attacked the women for their stubbornness. "At Carmaux . . . the movement for socialism and free thought is admirable, but if the movement is followed by almost all workers, unfortunately, their wives, imbued with prejudice . . . [and] infatuated with stupid superstitions, remain absolutely unmoved."[33] A civil burial for a woman was a rare occasion and when one occurred in 1892 the readers of *La Voix de Travailleurs* were assured that the deceased had requested it "voluntarily and in absolute possession of her mental faculties." This burial served as a rebuke to other wives of miners and glassworkers who prevailed on "the blameworthy weakness of their husbands" and continued to baptize their children and send them to religious schools.[34] Despite their wives' objections, however, large numbers of workers in Carmaux attended civil ceremonies and supported the movement against the church. In 1892 they formed a civil baptism society, retaining the social functions of godparents as protectors of a child while discarding all religious rites.[35] Throughout the 1890's, moreover, they elected candidates to municipal office who pledged to establish secular schools in Carmaux. Although wives of miners and glassworkers continued to separate personal attachments to religious ceremonies from social and political affiliations, they nonetheless supported and often engaged in strikes and political meetings with their husbands. Some even donned red dresses for particularly important occasions.

Weaknesses were usually tolerated for traditional religious practices associated with private events in one's life, whereas a man's political position was the crucial determinant of his place in the community of miners and glassworkers. Those who dissented shared the fate of glass-

worker Marius Rauzier. An outspoken and militant
organizer, Rauzier had been among the founders of the
glassworkers' union. He had traveled the country for the
Fédération du Verre and headed the general strike committee in 1891. As a municipal councillor he introduced
proposals for secularized schools and, an acknowledged
leader, he often addressed assemblages of miners and glassworkers. In 1892, Rauzier, along with Aucouturier and
others, opposed the candidacy of the "bourgeois intellectual Jaurès." But when others finally offered their
support, Rauzier refused to move. Charging that politics in
any form was less revolutionary than union action, he
nonetheless threatened to support Jaurès' opponent rather
than compromise his true principles.[36]

Pressure from the union leadership, but also from the
rank and file, who saw Jaurès as an ardent defender of their
rights, forced Rauzier to resign his union posts.[37] In response to "calumnious attacks" from Carmaux, the administrative council of the Fédération du Verre, voted their
support to Rauzier, finding that "he has not ceased to
(fight) for the proletarian cause."[38] But in January, the
Chambre syndical des verriers de Carmaux notified the
Federation that Rauzier had been replaced as its corre-
sponding secretary. After Jaurès' triumph in February, the
union gave Rauzier "a vote of full . . . confidence," but
refused to reelect him to any official post.[39] By mid-1893,
Rauzier found himself an outcast among the working
population. With his situation becoming more and more
"impossible," he moved his family from Carmaux to
Bordeaux.[40]

Rauzier's case suggested all the elements which organized
the glassworkers and miners into a coherent community. A

political dispute resulted in his ouster from the union. Refusal to support the designated socialist candidate disqualified him as a spokesman for the glassworkers. Having been denied further participation in the union, he became an outcast among the workers of Carmaux. If Rauzier had been involved merely in an argument among the socialist leadership, the attacks against him probably would have been as strong as they were. But his isolation from virtually the entire community would not have been so complete. "This dangerous leader," reported the police in January, 1893, "has left this city where he was excluded from the glassworkers' union."[41] Another official added that Rauzier had "lost his prestige among the glassworkers who considered him a sell-out."[42] If the glassworkers held this view, the miners almost inevitably shared it. Rauzier's departure from Carmaux was a physical manifestation of the "impossible" isolation he experienced. This kind of social cohesion as much as astute political organizing enabled Carmaux's socialists to mobilize strikes and to turn out the vote and triumph at the polls.

Socialist Electoral Politics

Traditionally, historians have attributed the introduction of socialism in Carmaux to the visit in 1882 of Paule Minck, an organizer for the Parti Ouvrier Français. She addressed a small meeting and encouraged the formation of a Cercle des Travailleurs, a workers circle or club. Although, for purposes of protection, its written rules prohibited all political and religious discussion, the club was probably dedicated to the "propagation of socialist ideas" and certainly to the initiation of trade unions. The twenty-six

founding members included twelve glassworkers, eight
miners, a former teacher, a carriage-maker, a mason, a
butcher, a barber, and a sculptor.[43] They aided in the
formal creation of a miners' union in 1884 and helped plan
the strikes of glassworkers and miners in 1882 and 1883.
The circle was dissolved in 1883, but some of its members
formed the nucleus of militant trade-union leadership in
Carmaux. For years they advocated working-class organization without winning much support. In 1892, they succeeded because their own efforts and propaganda coincided
with the needs and experiences of Carmaux's workers. The
program, the appeal, and the success of Carmaux's socialists
substantiate the argument of Bernard Moss that "labor
socialism" grew out of concrete experiences and was ultimately a pragmatic expression of working-class needs.[44]

In 1888, Carmaux's socialists joined the Fédération des
Travailleurs du Tarn, a loose alliance of various socialist
tendencies in the region, which published the first newspaper concerned solely with workers' problems, *La Voix
des Travailleurs*. The paper publicized the activities of the
socialist minority throughout the department and, by
presenting detailed information about employment opportunities and developments in various factories, it drew a
readership larger than the Federation's actual membership.

With the support of the Fédération des Travailleurs, two
glassworkers won seats on Carmaux's Municipal Council in
1888. One of them, Marius Rauzier, brother of a founder
of the Cercle, became a key figure in the glassworkers'
union when it formed in 1890.[45] In 1888, however, both
Rauzier and Petrus Charrier ran as individuals and spoke as
workers rather than as socialists.[46] In March, 1889, a
congress of the Fédération des Travailleurs decided unani-

mously "to run working-class candidates as a way of stating our demands."⁴⁷ The candidate chosen for the Conseil d' Arrondissement in Carmaux was a carpenter, Hippolyte Bouteillé.

Carmaux's representatives to the congress hoped to capitalize on the fact that Carmaux had been designated a canton early in 1889. (Prior to this time, the city had been a commune in the canton of Monestiès.) As a separate canton, Carmaux was composed of six communes: Carmaux, Blaye, St. Benoît, Rosières, Labastide-Gabausse, and Taix. Accordingly, with miners and glassworkers constituting the mass of the city's electorate (and with miners a large proportion of the populations of Blaye, St. Benoit, and Rosières), the Fédération des Travailleurs expected a significant margin of votes, if not a victory. Yet, on July 28, 1889, Bouteillé gained only 280 votes, far fewer than the 1392 and 985 votes cast for the two Republican candidates. The electoral potential for a socialist victory created by the administrative reorganization was not to be realized for another three years.⁴⁸

Bouteillé ran as a socialist, a term frequently used but barely defined by the leaders of the Fédération des Travailleurs. As if in recognition of the fact that Bouteillé's defeat indicated their own failure to offer a meaningful appeal to the potential constituency, Carmaux's socialists began to define socialism in terms workers could understand. In a remarkably nonpolitical editorial a spokesman from Carmaux called upon his comrades to unite. "What is a socialist?" he asked in the wake of Bouteillé's defeat in December, 1889. His answer stressed personal concerns and dealt with the same issues the unions might address:

He is a man who . . . wants to transform [society] in a more equitable direction . . . What does he want? . . . He wants justice for everyone . . . He wishes that the rich . . . were less selfish . . . and that those who give their strength, [and] their health, were better paid . . . What does he want to be? . . . He wants to be fairly paid for his work, to give an education to his family, to give food and necessary care to his old parents . . . because it is not just that those who have worked their whole lives have harvested only misery for their old age, while those who do not work possess everything . . .

Who of you dear friends is not a socialist after this exposé of reasons? All of you are, without exception.[49]

This piece might once have been written by a Republican. It was an appeal for social justice which contained no hint of class struggle or of social revolution. Yet the fact that these ideas were labeled socialist reveals a source of socialism's initial appeal to a working-class audience whose interests had not been served despite universal suffrage and the rhetroic of democracy. Jaurès stated it best in an electoral address in 1892. After listing the great accomplishments of the Republic he went on to its great failure: "Invaded by the monied powers it has adjourned the social question."[50] And it was the social question, in all its aspects, that preoccupied the socialist leadership of Carmaux. They began, after 1889, to raise issues relevant to life in the city that could not be treated within a strictly trade-union context.

Marius Rauzier did not press for higher pay or recognition of the union as a member of the Municipal Council; instead, he demanded the secularization of schools. This was, of course, a national issue and one supported by Republicans. But Carmaux's workers saw it as a problem which followed from their dependence on the Marquis de Solages. Solages long had provided funds for schools in Carmaux, but insisted that they be staffed by nuns and priests. When opposition to his religious schools arose, he simply threatened to withdraw his financial support. The issue became more pressing as Carmaux's population grew and as the enforcement of child labor laws further swelled the numbers of potential pupils. Not only were more buildings and teachers needed for workers' children, but the kind of education offered and the control of it was at stake. In insisting that the city, and not the Marquis, establish and support its own schools, Rauzier and others were asserting the right of Carmaux's residents to influence and control their town. The first vote on Rauzier's proposal was defeated in May, 1890, and he walked out of the meeting in protest. "I no longer want to be a part of a municipality" he announced "which calling itself Republican refuses to approve this just reform."[51] He reintroduced the question again in October with some success: The municipality voted to secularize one elementary school. In January, 1891, Rauzier joined left-Republicans and socialists in Carmaux in the new Société du Sou des Ecoles Laïques, a group devoted to raising money for and promoting the establishment of lay public schools.[52] The issue created great controversy. Parents of children at the religiously affiliated school petitioned to retain the nuns as instructors, but the council's resolution prevailed.[53] The question of secular schools, once a position synonymous with Republicanism, became a key plank in the worker's party platform for the municipal election of 1892, and, one by one, schools free of clerical domination were opened in Carmaux.

Another issue raised by the socialists and crucial to all

workers involved health. Though both the mines and glassworks provided some medical services, the socialists
argued that the city ought to establish free clinics and
hospitals and that it ought to reduce the price of medicine
at pharmacies. Other problems raised by union activity,
such as the glassworker strike of 1891, might best be solved
under municipal direction too. A sympathetic mayor would
not turn union membership lists over to police and could
refuse to send surveillance reports to the Prefect and to
Paris. And, above all, a city government which represented
their interests could help alleviate the burden on workers of
the high cost of living.[54] The miners struck in 1892 for
higher wages, but the increases they won seemed only a
partial solution. Land speculation and rents also had to be
controlled by a more vigilant city authority. And if municipal taxes on food were lowered and a progressive tax levied
for certain categories of housing, workers might better be
able to subsist. Strikes demanding higher wages began to
seem inadequate, and the socialist leaders directed an
increasingly receptive audience of miners and glassworkers
to electoral politics for a resolution of their problems.

The leadership of the unions began to speak at local
meetings and in newspaper articles of the need for powerful representation in the city government. One article
summed up their appeal: "The Republican government . . .
permits the mining company to keep in an iron yoke republican miners who have broken the chains of slavery and
crushed the despotic, clerical reaction. The Republican
government permits a mining company to stop the extrac-
tion of coal [and create] unemployment . . . Is this an
assurance and a guarantee of the miners' independence?"[55]
On a Sunday in December, 1891, a meeting of some 1000

miners and 400 glassworkers named a committee to choose
ten candidates to run in the complementary elections for
the municipal council. The ten would, in the words of a
participant, "hold firm and high in their calloused hands,
the flag of the social Republic."[56] On January 3, 1892, with
no other candidates running against them, the entire list
was elected. Only about half of Carmaux's eligible voters
deposited ballots in the urns and 100 of these were blank.
The socialist candidates received a maximum of 909 and a
minimum of 875 votes, almost triple the number cast for
Bouteillé in 1889.[57] Despite the fact that the election had
been uncontested, the socialists had good reason for
optimism. At least 50 percent of the electorate was willing
to vote for them.

With an important victory behind them, the socialists
began to prepare for the general municipal elections,
appropriately slated for May 1, 1892. They adopted as
their program the municipal platform which the Parti
Ouvrier Français had formulated at its Congress of Lyons
in 1891. The fourteen points (dealing with social services,
support of unions, and taxation) enumerated at Lyons
were remarkably suited to the concerns of miners and glassworkers in Carmaux and, for that matter to workers in
most cities in France. Undoubtedly, the party leaders
designed their program to win the votes of the growing and,
if Carmaux is representative, increasingly stable urban
workforces. The potential they knew existed must have
informed the Guesdist strategy in 1891–92, which defined
the city hall as the "base of operations" for the larger
socialist struggle. The strategy won the first great victories
for the Parti Ouvrier Français in the municipal elections of
1892 when Carmaux was one of twenty-two cities in which
a workers' slate triumphed.[58]

The significance of the May election could be seen in the number of votes the socialists secured. Many more people turned out to vote in May than had in January: abstentions dropped to about 34 percent. And clearly those who turned out came to vote socialist. Although the exact figures vary, Trempé's estimate that the socialists secured 1685 votes is probably correct. With only 16 percent more men voting, the number of socialist votes had nonetheless nearly doubled. In each of Carmaux's three electoral districts more than 60 percent of the votes went to the socialist list. And in the quartier Sainte Cécile, the newer section inhabited by miners recently settled in Carmaux, close to 75 percent of those eligible voted socialist.[59]

The capture of the Hôtel de Ville symbolized the solidarity of Carmaux's workers and it demonstrated the importance to them of municipal issues. Led by their unions, the miners and glassworkers joined together for the first time and cast their votes for their own representatives. In 1889, one socialist candidate had failed to rally a significant worker turnout; in 1892, he and every other man on the socialist list had taken the town in an election. The issues in the election had not merely drawn on vague dissatisfactions or an unspecified desire for reform. Rather, Carmaux's workers declared themselves socialists in 1892. The outgoing mayor reported long victory processions with women dressed in red, red flags and banners flying, the singing of the Carmagnole, and people shouting "notably in front of my house, 'down with the *bourgeoises*'."[60]

If there were any doubts that the election of 1892 expressed the determination of Carmaux's workers to control their town, the events that followed dispelled them. The new Municipal Council named as mayor Jean-Baptiste Calvignac, secretary of the miners' union, treasurer of the society for secular schools, an active member of the Fédération des Travailleurs, and an outspoken socialist. In August, 1892, Calvignac stood for the Conseil d'Arrondissement and defeated the Marquis de Solages's candidate, a M. Cabot. Whereas the election of May had demonstrated socialist strength within the city, this election illustrated its position in the entire canton. Within the city of Carmaux itself Calvignac won about 68 percent of the votes cast. The third district of Sainte Cécile gave him 74 percent of their votes. He won, too, in the communes of Blaye, Saint Benoît, and Rosières, all heavily populated by miners. Only in the agricultural communes of Taix and Labastide-Gabausse did Cabot manage to defeat Calvignac.[61]

Several days later, the mining company fired Calvignac for frequent and unauthorized absences from work. When the company refused Calvignac's request for two-days-a-week of leave to enable him to fulfill his official duties, the miner had taken the time off anyway. The company claimed that he was an irresponsible employee, and the miners replied that their leader's dismissal had only political motivation. They demanded that Calvignac be rehired and when the Director of the Mines refused to consider the question, the miners' union called a strike.[62]

The dispute raged from August 3 until November 15 and aroused the sentiments of the entire town. Although the glassworkers did not call a sympathy strike (financially, it would have been disastrous since large contributions from the glassworkers helped the miners to continue their strike), many joined the miners' activities. On August 15, a group of some 2000 workers invaded the home of the Director of the Mines to force the immediate satisfaction of their demands, calling for the Director's resignation or his head. One glassworker and nine miners were arrested during the disturbance and sentenced to one to four months in prison.[63]

Nominally a miners' strike, the defense of Calvignac was, in fact, an effort of "the entire population of Carmaux." The presiding judge at the trial in Albi accused all of the town of being "equally responsible as the ten accused" for the events which threatened the life of the Director of the Mines.[64] Bands of workers harassed the policemen and soldiers stationed in Carmaux and, on October 15, one group blocked a bridge, preventing police from approaching the company housing development for miners. Elected municipal officials also supported the workers. The mayors of Carmaux and of the communes of Blaye, St. Benoît, and

Table 17. Number of Votes Received in the Election to the Conseil d'Arrondissement, Canton of Carmaux, August, 1892

	Candidate	
Commune	Calvignac	Cabot
Carmaux		
First district	553	304
Second district	471	218
Third district		
(Ste. Cécile)	336	115
Blaye	238	181
St. Benoît	176	103
Rosières	112	64
Taix	28	36
Labastide-Gabausse	43	84
Total	2007	1110

Source: *La Voix des Travailleurs*, 4 août 1892.

Rosières refused to post the Prefect's order of October 11, 1892, prohibiting meetings or public gatherings of groups of more than 20.[65] The issues in the strike involved not merely Calvignac's job, but the rights of suffrage and control of the city as well. If the majority's choice for mayor was prevented by his employer from fulfilling the obligations of his office, the will of the electorate would be thwarted. According to Jaurès, who counseled the miners throughout the long strike, to national socialist leaders Duc-Quercy and Eugène Baudin, as well as to the strikers themselves, the strike represented an attempt to guarantee the political liberties of the voters of Carmaux. Paul Lafargue, an early organizer of the Parti Ouvrier Français went further, and defined the struggle as part of the larger "political and economic battle against the bourgeoisie." Most workers apparently agreed with him. They ended meetings throughout the strike with revolutionary oaths and songs. On October 7, some 2000 women, among whom a police officer noted "many wives of glassworkers with their children," paraded through the town. They carried four flags "of which at least one was entirely red," and shouted "the refrain of the Carmagnole: "Vive la sociale! Vive la révolution!"[66]

In November the dispute was settled by a compromise forced in the Chamber of Deputies by Baudin and Alexandre Millerand. Calvignac was given back his job and then granted a leave of absence. The ten prisoners were released and four of them were readmitted to the mines. When they emerged from the jail in Albi, the ten confronted a crowd of 10,000. Led by Baudin, Duc-Quercy, and Calvignac, the miners and glassworkers of Carmaux, joined by "diverse personalities of the socialist party of the Tarn", celebrated the successful defense of their representatives and of their right to a controlling voice in the municipal government.[67] The strike had ramifications in the Chamber of Deputies in Paris as well as in the city hall at Carmaux. The tremendous opposition to the Marquis de Solages generated by the strike led him to resign his seat in October, 1892. In the special election held in Januray, 1893, Jean Jaurès, who had worked closely with the miners during their long labor dispute, was elected as a socialist to represent the Tarn.[68] Jaurès was reelected in the general election held in August by an even greater margin than in January. An analysis of votes cast underscores the influence of socialism in Carmaux in 1893. The second district of Albi included four cantons in addition to Carmaux. Jaurès won in three of these, but most heavily in Carmaux, where he gained 2586 votes as opposed to his opponent's 921. It was this margin that insured his victory. Trempé has calculated that 45.4 percent of all Jaurès' votes came from the canton of Carmaux and that of these 92 percent came from the communes of Carmaux, Blaye, and Saint Benoît. Within the canton he secured 72.6 percent of the votes cast. In the city of Carmaux, the quartier Sainte Cécile again led the other two electoral districts by giving Jaurès 86 percent of its vote. The determination of the workers of Carmaux to send their representative to Parliament was demonstrated in another way too: only 16.1 percent of all eligible voters abstained.[69]

The overwhelming vote for Jaurès undoubtedly expressed the gratitude of Carmaux's workers for his role in the miners' strike. But it also expressed endorsement for the Parti Ouvrier Français platform which listed among its seventeen points issues of immediate concern to Carmaux's workers. The strike had demonstrated how little concern the Republic had for its workers. A government responsive to their needs would not have intervened against them in the recent strike. Indeed, the strike would never have occurred if more men like Jaurès set national policy and if national policy concerned itself with the interests of the working man. Jaurès' platform called for "the responsibility of employers for all accidents" (point 8), "the eight-hour day and a minimum wage" (point 9), "employee control of health and emergency funds" (point 13), "factory inspectors to be elected by union members" (point 15), and "old age and invalid assistance" (point 16).[70]

The strike and the election of Jaurès did not settle definitively the question of the socialists' control in Carmaux. In 1894 Calvignac's position as mayor was threatened again. In an effort to harass the socialists, the Prefect of the Tarn suspended him for an infraction of a regulation. Almost the entire Municipal Council resigned in protest and new elections were held in April, 1894. The socialist list easily won reelection and Calvignac again became mayor of Carmaux. Again the Prefect suspended him for a year and this time the Council accepted the decision. At the end of the year, the deputy mayor who had replaced Calvignac refused to relinquish the office. An angry Calvignac allegedly accused the deputy of betraying him. For this he was charged with insulting a municipal official and, in early 1895, the miner-leader was sentenced to forty days in prison and barred from holding office for five years. But in July, 1895, the workers of Carmaux defied judicial and government authorities and elected Calvignac and glassworker Marien Baudot to the general council of the canton. Of 2267 votes cast for each position, Calvignac received 1968 and Baudot 1862.[71]

By 1893 Carmaux's workers had claimed the city as their own and they had a representative to speak for them in Paris. Miners and glassworkers had "humiliated . . . the political and social power" of Solages and Rességuier. Labor had, however momentarily, triumphed over capital and a "seed of the social republic" had been planted in the region. During the strike of 1895, the glassworkers of Carmaux sent an appeal to "workers, socialists, and Republicans of France." They defined Rességuier's refusal to arbitrate their strike as an attack not only on the political strength of miners and glassworkers but as "the murder of a city which for several years had given everything . . . to the Republic and to the people."[72] The city of Carmaux and the community of workers within it had become synonymous.

In August, 1893, during an argument between some workers in a cafe, intervening police were beaten by onlookers. Several months earlier "anonymous crowds" threw garbage and insults at the Procurer of the Republic and a few policemen. Describing these events, a worried Prefect wrote of Carmaux to the Ministry of Interior, "today . . . the *gendarmes* are the objects of grave violence . . . a policeman's life is in danger . . . [t]he calm is only apparent . . . there is no longer safety for representatives of the law nor for agents of the mining company; [they] are deluged by a multitude which lacks all respect for them." The Prefect's fear was based on his recognition of an almost totally organized community of workers in Carmaux. Its strength lay in the fact that it contained the vast majority of the city's population and in its unity of values and of purpose. The Prefect's conclusion was shared not only by police and employers but also by the miners and glassworkers of the city: "Carmaux believes itself to be a state within the state."[73]

The Strike of 1895
6

As the miners' strike had expressed the solidarity of socialist strength in Carmaux in 1892, the glassworkers' strike of 1895 revealed one aspect of its ultimate weakness. The strike was only the second major one ever called by Carmaux's glassworkers since the founding of their union in 1890.[1] And it was their last. It climaxed five years of struggle for control of the factory between the union and Rességuier. During this time the glassworkers had redefined their conception of a union and thus implicitly accepted the transformation of their craft the union had originally been formed to prevent.

The Background

The only other strike of unionized glassworkers in Carmaux occurred in October, 1891. It was called by the national Fédération du Verre and deemed a "general strike" within the industry. The strike was not directed specifically at Rességuier but at all owners of glass bottle factories. It is important to examine this strike in some detail for it

provides a needed historical perspective for the strike of
1895.

Glassworkers had decided at their second congress
(Lyon's, September 1–6, 1891) to present a set of common
demands to their employers, the most important of which
was a demand for a unified wage scale. In part this demand
reprensented the Federation's desire to test its power as a
national body, and to test the effectiveness of a general
strike, the weapon called for at Lyons if employers failed
to satisfy their workers.[2] But it also was offered as a real
solution to problems of falling wages and unemployment.
If there were a unified wage scale, it was thought, there
would be less incentive for glassworkers to move to areas
where pay was better, where they competed with the
established glassworkers of the particular region or glassworks and drove down their wages. In effect, it made
"settling" more feasible than traveling. In addition, it permitted those glassworkers in higher paying establishments
to ask for increases on the basis of an even higher national
wage scale. A related point in the 1891 program asked that
the glassworkers themselves, rather than other auxiliary
workers, be permitted to break rejected bottles (those with
defects of one kind or another). The right to break rejects
meant the glassblower knew that his bottles were not being
sold as seconds (without his having been paid for them)
and allowed him to keep count of the number of satisfac-
tory bottles he blew and, therefore, of the wages owed him.

On September 21, 1891, representatives of the Fédération du Verre presented all forty-five owners of French
glass bottle factories with lists of the demands. Thirty-four
of the owners met in Paris on October 2 and rejected their
employees' ultimatum.[3] On October 6, the general strike

of French glassworkers began. The movement's headquarters were in Carmaux, where 400 glassworkers and an
equal number of auxiliaries, including women and children,
joined the strike. Marius Rauzier and Maximilien Charpentier, two leaders of Carmaux's union, collected funds and
directed the national effort. Carmaux's glassworkers struck
in support of their fellow workers rather than because of
specific grievances. They already enjoyed many of the
conditions set forth, and Rességuier was willing to concede
the demand for breaking rejects. Furthermore, Carmaux's
wage schedule was the model for the unified scale asked
by the Federation.

Carmaux's union supported the strike not only because
it subscribed to decisions of the Federation but also because it believed that a collective action of all souffleurs
(especially) could force the employers to comply. The
industry-wide strike of 1891, in this sense, involved a with-
drawal of skill by the most skilled, with support from
auxiliary workers. It sought higher wages and improved
conditions for all the strikers; a collective action was employed to satisfy all members of the collectivity. In this
sense, the local union and Federation were each no more
important than the sum of the glassworkers composing
them.

In Carmaux the strike continued until November 20. At
other establishments it lasted from two to fifty-one days,
and succeeded only partially at Montluçon, Rive-de-Gier,
St. Léger-des-Vignes, and Carmaux. In these cases success
consisted of the implementation of some demands like the
one for an eight-hour day, or a day of rest every week, or
the "breaking of rejects" at Carmaux. The overall goal of a
single wage schedule failed everywhere.[4]

Although they constantly endorsed the tactic of a general strike, the Federation never again called one after 1891. The joint force of their employers had proved superior to their own, and the economic situation in the industry favored the employers as well. Regional conditions were too diverse, some unions were more powerful than others and could more successfully obtain concessions from individual owners. In fact, at Carmaux, the strike had really benefited Rességuier, who used the opportunity to get rid of some of his oversupply. Indeed, he seemed to have come out so far ahead that some union members retrospectively accused his agents of fomenting the entire general strike.[5]

As it pursued negotiations with Rességuier after 1891, the union came to represent more than an instrument of control for the souffleurs. Their skill as craftsmen became secondary in achieving the souffleurs' aims. More important were the skill of union representatives in bargaining with Rességuier, the organization the union gave to the factory, the financial resources it had, and its ability to mobilize not only every rank of glassworker but other workers and small tradesmen in the city. The institution of the union came to be seen as the only means of attaining the glassworkers' ends. "The union is a school . . . not a grouping of professionals," wrote Marien Baudot in 1894, "where the worker ought to come to study, with his brothers in misery, the surest and most practical means to rid himself of oppression."[6]

In 1894 when a souffleur wanted a job for his nephews, he asked the union's permission. Committees and councils weighed the problem, a general assembly resolved other issues. The "support of the union" was asked by some grands garçons seeking promotion, not the support of their comrades, or even of union *members*.[7] The union no longer represented skill alone but a force with the power of numbers, with an internal organization which gave it control over punishing apprentices for not paying dues and which gave it a personality that could be insulted and could seek revenge. By 1895, when one of its leaders was fired by Rességuier, the union responded by declaring a strike. There were several issues in the strike of 1895, but the fact that protection of a fellow worker was a primary motive, rather than wages or working conditions, was most important. When, several months earlier, Rességuier reinstituted the practice of selling rather than breaking imperfect bottles his glassworkers had considered striking but decided against it. Instead, the union announced that it had "decided to temporarily accept the conditions imposed by the administrator . . . [but it] protests against this measure which hurts . . . [glassworkers] wages."[8] When, however, Rességuier fired Marien Baudot, for obvious political reasons, the union took immediate action. An action against one union member, particularly a leader, meant that the existence of the union itself was threatened. (And, indeed as will be seen in the following pages, the actions and statements of Rességuier indicated that he intended to destroy the union.)[9] The fact that what was at stake was protection of the union (and not status or skill) sustained, and strengthened, but also ultimately defeated the glassworkers' strike of 1895.

The Strike of 1895

On July 30, 1895, Marien Baudot received notice of his dismissal from the Verrerie Sainte Clothilde. He was charged with having absented himself from work without

1. Main entrance to the Verrerie Sainte Clothilde, 1895.

permission. From July 21 to 27, Baudot had attended the congress of the Fédération du Verre at Marseilles. As was the custom at the glass factory, he had registered before his departure with the man who organized work schedules. Any glassworker who did not want to or could not work merely notified this man, who then arranged for a replacement. The replacement came from a group of glassworkers who constituted the *relai* or reserve force and who served only as substitutes for regular employees. There were no penalties for absences from work except the voluntarily incurred loss of wages.[10] Rességuier claimed that although Baudot had followed proper procedure, the nature of his absence demanded special permission. It was one thing if a worker were tired or ill, but quite another if he deserted the factory on union business.

As long as the union aided Rességuier within the glassworks, he had allowed it to exist. Relying on the skill and standards of his souffleurs, he permitted them to supervise the hiring and firing of employees. The union enforced factory discipline as well as union regulations and, as a result, Rességuier found his plant more efficiently run. But, although the Director permitted the union a certain control at the factory, he never defined the areas of its authority. From its foundation in 1890, the union engaged in a continual struggle with Rességuier. After the strike of 1891, the union demanded that its representatives be allowed to determine which bottles were to be rejected for imperfections; Rességuier countered that it was his right. The union insisted on setting the numbers of workers needed at the factory; Rességuier, as director, felt he had the right to decide how many to employ. The union organized an insurance fund (to be used in case of a strike as well as to

145

aid sick workers and their families); Rességuier maintained that all glassworkers must contribute to his fund. Finally, by 1895, the Director found the union's demands becoming "intolerable" and he determined "to prove that he knew how to be the master of his house." According to one of his vice-presidents, he decided to "break . . . the union" to accomplish his end.[11]

Rességuier's design involved a good deal more than the reassertion of control over the administration of his factory. As the union became an increasingly political organization, it threatened his political position in Carmaux and in the department of the Tarn. In fact, since 1892, the heads of the glass factory and the mining company had forged a coalition of conservatives in a drive to recapture Carmaux's votes. But on July 28, 1895, Marien Baudot was elected to the Conseil d'Arrondissement, despite the fact that he, like Calvignac, had been declared ineligible for office. His election represented a defeat for Rességuier and his allies and a defiance of prefectural and judicial authority by the socialist glassworkers and miners of the city. By firing Baudot on July 30, then, Rességuier indicated that union business and, especially, political activity, conflicted with the responsibilities of a souffleur. The firing of Baudot struck not only at the behavior of one individual. It was an explicit attack on the increasingly political trade unionism and militant socialist politics of most glassworkers at the Verrerie Sainte Clothilde.

The glassworkers rallied to protect Baudot by calling a strike. Initially a gesture of protest, the strike quickly became a battle for the union's survival. The stake for both Rességuier and the union was much the same—control over the conditions of work. At issue were the employer's authority and the rights of his employees. Moreover, each side sought to demonstrate that it was the ultimate source of and had the ultimate right to economic and political control. While Rességuier maintained that ownership and economic enterprise gave him authority over his employees and entitled him to political power, the union insisted that workers were entitled to their jobs and to control of their work. But for the workers the power to enforce these rights stemmed only from their collective action and organization.

The union's decision to call a strike on July 31 constituted a significant departure from previous policy. When Rességuier had announced in May, 1895, that he could no longer abide by his agreement of 1891 to break defective bottles, the union protested. But it did not strike. The glassworkers well knew that Rességuier's warehouses were overstocked with bottles and that a work stoppage would only enable him to get rid of his surplus stock. He could afford and even profit from a strike. For them, however, it would mean only hardship. Rességuier declared that as of June, he would sell the least defective of rejects as "seconds" and, further, that the glassworkers would receive half-pay for each "second" they produced. The union delegates protested that since most rejects were unusable the choice of seconds would be made among perfect bottles, in effect lowering a glassworker's wages. After several arbitration sessions, Rességuier conceded a maximum of twenty-five "seconds" a day. The union insisted that this far surpassed the usual number of rejects, but it reluctantly agreed to accept the concession. By a vote of 192 to 83, the glassworkers of Carmaux decided not to strike. Instead they protested by publicly "revealing" the real intent of Rességuier's new policy. It was, they proclaimed, simply a guise by which to lower the wages of his workers.[12]

In July, Rességuier held his position of economic

strength—he still had a large surplus of bottles. But in his attack on Baudot, he had attacked the very existence of the union." On the question of salary, we accepted . . . but . . . on the dismissal of our comrade . . . our conscience, our honor, our concern for the Republic and for socialism forbid our bending or compromising."[13] Baudot had been a union delegate sent by the glassworkers to represent them at a national congress and he had been elected by workers to represent Carmaux in the district council. He stood for what they stood for, he was not a leader, one who stood above and apart, but a "comrade . . . invested with union functions." Not surprisingly, then, Carmaux's glassworkers perceived the discharge of Baudot as an attack on themselves. "In striking [him] you strike us all" they charged Rességuier.[14] The "us all" moreover, was corporate, not individual. Lowered wages hit many individual pockets, but firing Baudot constituted "systematic warfare against all working class organization and all social emancipation." "The truth is that by hitting at those you call leaders you hope that in the future, none of your workers will dare fill a union office. Or serve on committees sent to you."[15] The glassworkers charged that by declaring that union business interfered with the work of the souffleur, Rességuier, in effect, had outlawed the union and violated the rights of association of his employees. By outlawing the union, he destroyed the focal point of his workers' political and social power, the organizing institution of their lives.

To defend the union, as much as to save Baudot, the glassworkers voted to strike on July 31. At seven in the evening no one from the night shift appeared at the factory. The Director ordered the fires extinguished and a four-month strike began. The next day, Jean Jaurès and several

members of the National Federation of Glassworkers
arrived in Carmaux. They advised the union to seek arbitration and to end the strike as quickly as possible. The stock
of bottles strengthened Rességuier's position (as it had in
May) and a long strike, as much as the firing of Baudot,
threatened to destroy the union. On August 2, the union
nominated five delegates and asked the Justice of the
Peace to set up a committee of conciliation (in accord with
provisions of the law of December, 1892). The application
for arbitration asked that Baudot's case be judged for
fairness since he had broken no rule. And it charged that
Baudot had been fired for political reasons "because he
[is] a militant socialist."[16]

Rességuier refused to arbitrate. He maintained that
questions of factory discipline ought to remain in the hands

2. Jaurès leads striking glassworkers to the Place Gambetta,
Carmaux, 1895.

of the employer. If they did not, the functioning of the factory would be impaired and all "industry would be weakened." Arbitration of an issue that properly belonged to an employer would set a dangerous precedent for all of French industry. Rességuier insisted that questions of hiring and firing be left to employers—in that realm, at least, control ought to be absolute. "The choice of personnel ought to belong to each [employer]. To do otherwise would be to interfere with a primordial right."[17] The right he referred to was the right of individual liberty and he declared that the union interfered not only with his freedom to choose his own workers but with a worker's freedom to negotiate individual arrangements with his employer. By claiming that he acted in the interest of his workers as well as of himself and by appealing to the courts for enforcement of "liberté du travail", Rességuier announced his intention to disband the union. He defined his role as a defender of individual liberty (and of French business interests) against its enemy, "association."

On August 6, the union reevaluated its tactical position in the light of Rességuier's refusal to negotiate and of his superior economic position. The glassworkers voted overwhelmingly to resume work. They decided to set up a fund to support Baudot, who would continue as secretary of the union. By redefining the issue as unjust punishment of an individual worker, the strategists (with Jaurès and Claussé, secretary of the national Federation) hoped to avert a direct attack on the union itself. But it was too late. Rességuier replied that since the glassworkers had left work "without cause" the factory would remain closed indefinitely.[18] He did not know when or under what conditions production would resume. At this point the strike became a "lock-out." Two weeks later, the administrators of the factory extended offers of employment to individual workers. Rességuier maintained that his factory was open to anyone wishing to work and to abide by his terms. He flatly rejected the union's demands that everyone be rehired collectively and that the Director guarantee the continued existence of the union and of wage levels. Such demands, he insisted, violated his freedom of choice. The union replied that its members wished to work but that Rességuier had locked them out in order to destroy the union and to lower their pay without opposition. He "is on strike against us, we want to work."[19] By refusing to acknowledge either the union's demands or its offer to resume production, Rességuier simply denied its legitimacy as a bargaining agent for his glassworkers. The principle of liberté du travail would be implemented by establishing separate relationships between each worker and his employer. Rességuier acted as if the union did not exist, in order to drive it out of existence. "He strikes at our most sensitive point," the spokesman for the union charged, "our spirit of solidarity."[20]

Yet it was precisely that spirit of solidarity, the strength of their collective experience and their consciousness of it that enabled the glassworkers to resist Rességuier as long as they did. At the beginning of the strike, 580 verriers (of whom 165 were souffleurs, 100 were porteurs, and the rest grands garçons and gamins), 218 auxiliaries, and 187 women were employed at the Verrerie Sainte Clothilde.[21] The administration's recruiting drive began on August 20. At the end of the month some 80 workers had negotiated individual contracts with Rességuier. But production could not be resumed at even one furnace since none of the 80 was a souffleur. By October 15 (two and one-half months after the strike began) only eight souffleurs had returned to the factory. The strength of the strike, like that of the union, rested on the unity of the most highly skilled glassworkers.[22]

The union's tight organization and the extensiveness of its influence reinforced the strike effort. Funds collected over the years and supplemented by donations from the national Federation and other groups were distributed regularly among the strikers and their families. Those who returned to the factory received no assistance, and the strikers kept a careful watch to determine which among them were "renegades." If, for some reason, a striking glass-worker had to go into the factory he was accompanied by

3. Striking glassworkers leaving their union hall, October, 1895.

a member of the strike committee. At the trial of a union
leader charged with interfering with liberté du travail, the
judge questioned a glassworker about the practice. "Why
did you request company [to go into the factory] . . .
Don't you care about your liberty?" The worker replied,
"Yes, but I care a great deal more about the esteem of my
comrades."[23]

The cohesiveness of the glassworking community which
had developed over a period of years was intensified during
the strike. Although esteem and "fraternity" characterized
relationships among strikers, those who violated comradeship were ostracized, threatened, and publicly abused. In
October, Antoine Savy decided to go back to the Verrerie
Sainte Clothilde. When his intention became known, he
was driven from a meeting and expelled from the union.
When the strikers met him on the street they shouted
"traitor," and one warned, "in a menacing tone, 'if you go
back to work, I will cut off your balls'."[24] Wives of
striking glassworkers often gathered in front of the factory,
cursing those who reported for work and offering them
bread as well. On October 4, Marie Vedel was arrested for
having yelled to four men entering the glassworks, "if you
are going to work because you need bread, we will give you
bread."[25] One striker, Louis Combelles, even had his
brother, Adrien, arrested, because in an argument about
the strike, Adrien, who had returned to work, hit Louis.[26]
In addition, the tension between the strikers and those few
who began to return to the Verrerie Sainte Clothilde was
exacerbated by the normal antagonism between souffleurs
and their apprentices, between glassworkers and auxiliaries.
The workers who brought charges against strikers (auxiliaries and apprentices for the most part) testified bitterly

to receiving threats and insults from those who felt themselves "superior" to auxiliary workers, from those with greater skill but far less dedication and service to the company.

Defections from the ranks of the strikers were few, however, in contrast to the widespread support not only from glassworkers but from other residents of Carmaux. On August 15, the miners donated 500 francs to the glassworkers' fund and voted, in addition, to give one day's pay each month as long as the strike continued.[27] Shopkeepers extended credit to the best of their working-class customers and contributed generously to the strike fund.[28] Jaurès and other socialist leaders toured the country to raise money, and many glassworker unions sent frequent messages of fraternal and financial support. Mayors of socialist municipalities allocated special gifts for the glassworkers of Carmaux and several newspapers undertook fund-raising drives. The money collected enabled the glassworkers to continue the strike without excessive hardship. And, their solidarity prevented Rességuier from reopening the glass factory on his terms.

By October, Rességuier was forced to turn to new measures in his effort to break the strike. He began recruiting workers from other towns and particularly from Rive-de-Gier, where a strike in 1894 had left many unemployed and where an effort to establish a cooperative was floundering. Often his agents reported to potential recruits that the strike at Carmaux was over but that additional staff was needed anyway. Finally, on October 2, Rességuier announced that he had hired enough glassworkers to resume production at one furnace. He requested that the Prefect send a force of gendarmes to Carmaux to guarantee the "liberty" of his new employees. During the next few days, the police began systematically arresting any strikers who seemed to be disturbing the peace.

Until October, Carmaux had been peaceful and neither side had been able to force the other to submit. The union had demonstrated its ability to survive and Rességuier had indicated his intention to run his factory his own way. After two months of strike, Rességuier called for reinforcements in the form of political pressure from the government. The Prefect of the Tarn, as well as some officials in Paris, seized the opportunity to move against a socialist municipality, to destroy the socialists' strength in Carmaux, and to discredit Jaurès. The forces of state power combined with Rességuier in an attack on the "state within the state." Denouncing this tactic as dangerous because it mixed political and professional interests, the vice-president of the administrative council of the glassworks, M. Sirven, resigned his position. "In reality," he wrote, ". . . it is impossible to see in this strike anything but a calculation of [Rességuier's] interest onto which a small political enterprise has been grafted."[29]

The police made fifteen arrests during the month of October for rebellion and interference with liberty. Maximilien Michon was sent to jail for three months; Michel Aucouturier was fined 500 francs and sentenced to four months in prison.[30] During the trials, endless numbers of glassworkers were called to testify and were themselves harassed and threatened by the prosecutor in the course of their testimonies. The most disastrous arrest was made on October 15. Maximilien Charpentier was charged with having interfered with liberté du travail. He had furnished money for railway passage to glassworkers who, when they learned they had been recruited to Carmaux to break a strike, wanted to return to their homes. When Charpentier, the treasurer of the union, was arrested, the entire strike fund was seized as well. Deprived of leadership and financial resources and demoralized by Rességuier's apparent success in attracting replacements for them, more and more strikers began to return to the factory.

More subtle pressures than arrests were exerted by the Prefect. During his daily tour of the town, the Prefect frequently paid calls on the families of recalcitrant glassworkers. Once he offered Agnès Dumas, an unemployed school teacher, a position if her glassworker father and brother agreed to Rességuier's terms. Another day he threatened to arrest the sister-in-law of Mme Bouteillé for having shouted insults at newly employed workers

4. The strike committee, October, 1895. (At center, with cigarette, Michel Aucouturier.)

unless her sons returned to the factory. A soldier was promised an extended leave of absence in return for breaking the strike and one glassworker, whose father-in-law worked for the railroad Compagnie du Midi, was told that his relative would be fired unless he (the glassworker) reappeared at the Verrerie Sainte Clothilde.[31] Jaurès charged, in the Chamber of Duputies, that the Prefect had gone beyond the call of duty in these cases, and he maintained that such government interference in a labor disupte was unjustified. In turn, local officials cited Jaurès as the instigator of the entire dispute, as the real force behind the glassworkers' "rebellion." At one point during Aucouturier's trial, the prosecutor turned on Jaurès who was observing the proceedings as a spectator. "It is this man, gentlemen," he called to the jury, "who has perverted the minds of the workers by his unreasonable ideas, and who, by his presence here . . . has attempted to put unfair pressure on the court."[32] Rességuier added further to the unfavorable publicity by suing Jaurès and two newspapers for 100,000 francs for having planned a conspiracy against him.

The strikers continued their resistance throughout October. Delegates went to glass centers throughout France and sometimes successfully dissuaded Rességuier's recruits from going to Carmaux. The national Federation called for a boycott of the Verrerie Sainte Clothilde, and Jaurès interpellated the government on October 24 on the behavior of the Prefect of the Tarn. Although the Chamber turned down Jaurès' proposal that its president arbitrate the conflict in Carmaux, the new ministry which came to power early in November did offer to seek a compromise. But with three furnaces now in operation and with new groups of glassworkers arriving each day, Rességuier again refused to negotiate. As he had in August he again insisted that "it is my right and I imagine that no arbitration will deprive me of this right, especially since I have hired no foreign workers; the choice of personnel ought to belong to every [employer]."[33]

On November 9, 850 striking glassworkers and auxiliaries met to discuss their plans. They called for the legal protection of unions and then they decided to establish a cooperative glassworks which would employ those fired by Rességuier. Although the meeting ended with cries of "Vive la grève," the glassworkers had concluded that they must end their strike. They vowed to continue their "struggle" until they had "obtained or created the necessary guarantees" for their trade union, but the founding of a "verrerie aux verriers" indicated that the struggle would be transformed.[34] In October, a wealthy philanthropist had given 100,000 francs toward the founding of a cooperative glass factory. By November 9, the Carmausins seized the offer as the only way out of the strike. Establishing a cooperative would enable militant glassworkers to continue working and would permit the existence of the union in a new establishment.

After November 9, glassworkers began to return to the factory in large numbers and on November 22 the strike was officially ended. Rességuier published a list of priorities for employment which indicated how complete a victory he had won. Again refusing to collectively reinstate the strikers he offered to rehire only 67 immediately. Two hundred thirty-eight names comprised a second category of glassworkers who would be called when Rességuier needed them. Another 78 were told they might possibly be rehired. Twenty-one glassworkers, the leaders of the union and socialist organizations, the members of the strike committee, were fired. Of the 480 souffleurs, grands garcons, and gamins who went on strike in August, only 67 were guaranteed jobs at the Verrerie Sainte Clothilde.[35] Almost the entire union membership and its supporters were dismissed by Rességuier. If the union insisted on its corporate identity, he would disband the union by firing its members and replacing them with glassworkers willing to conceive of themselves as individuals. This measure, ironically, demonstrated the strength of the glassworkers' solidarity. Rességuier could not disband the union. He had to fire all its members to rid his factory of its influence.

Yet Rességuier's victory also demonstrated the ultimate futility of the glassworkers' cause. He could fire every souffleur in his factory because they were easily replaced by cheaper, less skilled, and less demanding workers. For this reason, although the strike of 1895 was the high point of the glassworkers' militancy it was also the last such action they undertook. It represented not only the defeat of the union on an immediate issue but the ultimate defeat of the souffleurs. And it revealed the contradiction embodied in the notion of the union expressed in Charpentier's speech of 1895. Though consciousness of the need for solidarity had enabled the glassworkers to resist Rességuier for several months, the impossibility of the goal of saving their positions as craftsmen meant they would inevitably lose the strike of 1895.

After the Strike

If it was not the ultimate cause of the defeat of the glassworkers' union, the strike of 1895 was nonetheless a turning point. After the strike no union existed at the

Verrerie Sainte Clothilde for more than a decade, and, with
the removal of the militant glassworkers to Albi, the
strength of Carmaux's socialists weakened as well.
Initially, the organizers of the cooperative glassworks
intended to build it in Carmaux directly across from the
Verrerie Sainte Clothilde. There it would stand as a symbol
of the strength of working-class opposition to Rességuier's
capitalism. After consultation with economists and engineers, however, it was decided that Albi, ten miles to the
south, was a better location. There the Verrerie Ouvrière
could be built along the railroad line and it would have fuel
from less antagonistic (and less expensive) sources than the
Solages mines. In this way it would eventually compete
successfully with Rességuier. Only by successfully competing with him would the cooperative demonstrate the
superiority of socialist principles to capitalism and the
ultimate justice of the glassworkers' cause. In addition, of
course, only successful competition would insure continued
employment for the former employees of Rességuier.[36]

When the decision to go to Albi was announced, the
miners decried the betrayal of the working-class community in Carmaux. "We do not know how to describe
the spectacle of this angry crowd," reported *La Dépêche
de Toulouse*. There were cries and shouts of protest. "Even
Baudin . . . whom all of Carmaux loves . . . whom all
militants . . . consider their friend and leader . . . even
Baudin . . . could not calm their anger." Calvignac resigned
and then "one after the other the delegates of the socialist
municipal councils of Blaye, Rosières, St. Benoît and
Carmaux came forward to resign [from the Republican-
socialist committee of the second district of Albi]."[37]
The miners blamed Jaurès and the glassworker leaders for

sacrificing fraternity to economy. If the glassworkers left Carmaux, the miners charged, the "general interest of the socialist party" would be sacrificed and the city would no longer represent "the advanced citadel of the entire party."[38] "What will it mean to have Carmaux's glassworks at Albi?" asked one irate miner leader. He answered his own question, "The triumph of the radical party over the socialist party."[39]

The uproar over the building of the cooperative at Albi indicated the socialists' perception of the importance of the militant glassworkers to working-class politics in Carmaux. And the tone of disappointment and the sense of betrayal expressed by the miners indicated the depth of communal feeling that had grown up among workers and the identification of that feeling with the city of Carmaux itself. Although Marien Baudot defended the move by insisting that national socialist interests be considered before "discussions of local interest" or of "personal questions," he nonetheless promised that the glassworkers of Albi would "remain closely united" with their comrades in Carmaux. He ended his appeal by charging that "certain opportunists and reactionaries are seeking . . . to divide . . . the workers of Carmaux" by fomenting discord over the location of the Verrerie Ouvrière.[40] Baudot's article concluded by affirming what he initially denied. Though he maintained that larger socialist interests must take precedence over local socialist issues, he, like the miners, defined the glassworkers' socialism in terms of Carmaux. Close links would be maintained between Albi and Carmaux; the glassworkers would continue to support the miners and "the workers of Carmaux" would remain united. "The workers of Carmaux" referred to both groups, to the socialist miners who lived there and to the departing glassworkers. The sense of community and the class identification of miners and glassworkers had made Carmaux a "citadel" of socialism. And its socialist inhabitants identified themselves as Carmausins. Thus the departure of so many militant glassworkers and of the union, even to a city as near as Albi, was perceived by the miners as a "total misunderstanding of the rights" and needs of the socialist community of Carmaux.[41]

In part, the miners were right, for 1895 did mark a turning point in the political life of Carmaux. Although the glassworkers came in a body from Albi to vote in the cantonal election in January, 1896, they could not continue to vote in Carmaux. In part, the loss of these votes contributed to the socialist loss of control of city politics to the radical party and to the Solages-Reille-inspired group, the Cercle Républican Progressiste. It also contributed to Jaurès' defeat in 1898 in the contest with Solages for his seat in the Chamber of Deputies.[42] Rességuier's victory in 1895 thus seemed complete. He had not only rid himself of a troublesome organization and of his surplus stock of bottles but of his political foes as well. After 1895 labor conflict subsided, socialist candidates did not always win elections, and Carmaux was no longer a "state within the state."

Yet it was not the loss of numerical strength which really destroyed the unity of Carmaux's working-class community. The glassworkers never accounted for more than 5 percent of the electorate, while the miners constituted more than half of the voting population of the city. Furthermore, the socialists not only lost the old glassworkers, they failed to attract many of the new recruits to the Verrerie Sainte

Clothilde. In addition, and more significant, they lost the
support of many miners as well. In part this was directly
related to the strike of 1895, for many miners were bitterly
disillusioned at the loss both of their comrades and of new
job opportunities for their sons. They denounced and
continued to blame the political opportunism of certain
glassworkers and of Jaurès. The Solages-Reille group took
advantage of the miners' bitterness and played on it in
their posters and election appeals. They also sent hecklers
who occasioned fights at meetings Jaurès held in Carmaux.
In these fights many of Jaurès' supporters were arrested.
This strategy led to Jaurès' defeat in the election of 1898.
He gained a majority only in the city of Carmaux and even
there it was a very slim majority of 99 votes. (This compared with his majority of 1370 in August, 1893, and his
future majority of 878 in 1902.) After that election there
continued to be a relative decline in socialist strength in
Carmaux. Whereas from 1893 to 1914, the number of
eligible voters increased by 28.6 percent and the number
of voters increased by 29.9 percent, the number of socialist
voters increased only by 11.7 percent.[43]

The decline in socialist electoral strength, however, did
not stem primarily from the miners' anger about the
Verrerie Ouvrière. Nor was it caused by the departure for
Albi of the militant glassworkers. Rather, just as the loss of
the strike of 1895 stemmed from occupational changes the
glassworkers could not control, so the defeat of the socialists was evidence of a profound structural transformation
which affected the unions as well. The weakening of the
socialist party coincided with a precipitous decline in miner
and glassworker union membership after 1895, a decline
so severe that union leaders described it as a "crise

syndicale."[44] According to Trempé, "The strength of the [miner's] union reached its apogee during the years 1892 to 1894." By 1899, she continues, "the miners were divided into two camps, ferociously hostile in their opposition to one another."[45] Even then, the membership of the two unions combined did not equal that of the single union in 1892. In fact, the rate of union membership for miners in Carmaux dropped from 93 percent in 1892 to 25 percent in 1896 to 17 percent in 1897.[46] Although in part the drop in membership came from the increasingly determined opposition of the company, this was not the whole explanation. The directors of the mines had provided continuing opposition to the union in the early 90's, too, but they had

Table 18. Unions of Glassworkers in France, 1884–1900

Year	Number of unions	Number of members
1884	9	717
1885	10	777
1886	10	777
1887	11	892
1888	11	892
1889	14	1084
1890	22	1064
1891	43	4799
1892	43	5701
1893	44	6778
1894	45	7352
1895	40	7143
1896	33	4064
1897	22	1925
1900	23	2913

Source: Direction du Travail, *Les Associations professionnelles ouvrières*, III, 518–519 (auxiliaries' unions are included).

met with determined resistance on the part of the miners. Clearly, after 1895 the union no longer seemed to miners a feasible or necessary instrument for dealing with their problems in the mines. Instead, they began leaving the mines in search of better jobs.

Similarly, the new glassworkers continued to reject offers of assistance and encouragement from their predecessors to form a union. In fact, they remained decidedly hostile to militancy in any form. Although, as with the miners, the opposition of their employer played a part in discouraging unionization after 1896, the fact that the situation in

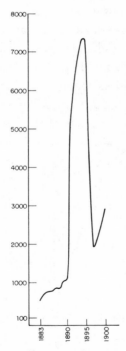

3. Members of the national federation of glassworkers, 1883–1900.

Source: Les Associations des professionelles ouvrières, III, 518–519.

Carmaux reflected the national situation among glassworkers indicates that more was at issue than fear of a
single employer. Whereas from 1890 to 1895 the number
of members of glassworker unions grew dramatically, after
1895, it dropped suddenly, and by 1897 membership had
fallen to the level of 1890[47] Interestingly, the graph of
membership in the national Federation of glassworkers
almost exactly parallels that of the miners' union in
Carmaux.

The decline in union membership and in socialist support
was directly related to the passing of the occupational
crises which had simultaneously affected the lives of both
miners and glassworkers and had transformed them into
militant socialists. As changes in work experiences had
stimulated the militancy of 1890–1895, so other changes in
the backgrounds and expectations of the workers would
be largely responsible for the decline of such militancy in
Carmaux in the closing years of the nineteenth century.

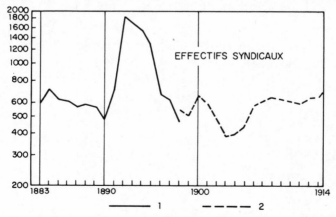

4. Members of the miners union of Carmaux, 1883–1914.
1 = 1er syndicat des ouvriers mineurs, 1883–1893
2 = 2^{e} syndicat des ouvriers mineurs, 1898–1914
Source: Rolande Trempé, *Les Mineurs de Carmaux*, 968.

After 1896, two glass factories existed in the Tarn. The Verrerie Sainte Clothilde at Carmaux continued as before, and Rességuier adopted stringent measures to prevent the organization of a new union among his workers. The Verrerie Ouvrière d'Albi, staffed by Rességuier's former employees and joined by socialists and dedicated cooperators from all over France, set out to prove the feasibility of association.

With the formation of their own factory, the glassworkers transformed a struggle between an employer's authority and the rights of his employees into a competitive conflict between two factories. "Before the unshakeable stubbornness of a despotic employer," wrote Jaurès describing the Verrerie Ouvrière, "the idea frequently has recurred that one could oppose factory to factory and [thus] strike at the interests and the pride of a reactionary and violent industrialist."[1]

The founders differed among themselves about the ultimate value of a cooperative. The Guesdists argued that such an undertaking could only develop revolutionary consciousness, but that it was not a viable means of transforming society. Others replied that by its example and the experiences of its members, a cooperative factory was in fact a means of resolving "the social problem." Whether defined as "an arm of defense"[2] against Rességuier or as a means of transforming society, the ultimate proof of the value of "association" lay in successful competition measured in standard economic terms. When "association" and "capitalism" were each embodied in a factory, traditional standards of production and profit defined failure or success. As a writer in *La Voix des Travailleurs* urged, "the first duty of those supporting [the Verrerie Ouvrière] is to seize every economic advantage, however minimal it appears . . . Above all it is important that a political victory . . . be complemented and confirmed by an economic victory."[3] The Verrerie Ouvrière eventually achieved an economic victory. It employed men who would otherwise have been unemployed and it also held its own in competition with the Verrerie Sainte Clothilde. But it neither won the battle for the right of association within Rességuier's factory nor did it fashion a revolutionary socialist institution. Instead, it increasingly resembled its competitor as old methods of production were discarded and as old glassworkers were succeeded by new ones.

* * * * *

Despite the fact that the glass factories at Albi and Carmaux embodied antithetical economic and social principles, both experienced similar developments between 1896 and 1914. The influx of a new type of worker, which had begun in the 1880's, accelerated as new machines finished the process which reduced the work of artisan glassblowers to that of semiskilled factory operatives.

One of the objections to locating the cooperative glass factory at Albi instead of in Carmaux involved the future of miners' sons. "What will become of all the sons of miners and cultivators who, for two or three or four years have worked at the Verrerie?" asked "a citizen" in a letter to *La Voix des Travailleurs.* Unable to travel to Albi each day, too poor to afford to board there, and too young to be deprived on the "care, which only a mother could give them," they would remain unemployed in Carmaux. The "sons of militant miners" especially, would suffer, since they had no hope of being hired at the mines. A Verrerie Ouvrière at Carmaux would have "permitted them to be apprenticed without great expense." Some might even have become glassblowers, others masons or adjusters at the cooperative. Finally, the letter dismissed out of hand the notion that Rességuier would employ "all these young men."[4]

Though the writer's prediction proved inaccurate, he did furnish an apt description of the background of the young men aspiring to enter the glassworks. In the years after 1896, both Rességuier and the Verrerie Ouvrière increasingly recruited their workers from the families of miners, peasants, common laborers, and petty craftsmen (such as the hatmakers of Albi) whose trades were waning or had disappeared. In the decade before the strike of 1895, 18 percent of the glassworkers married in Carmaux were born in the department of the Tarn. Yet, after the strike, between 1896 and 1905, 61 percent of those glassworkers married listed the Tarn as their birthplace. (See Table B.) Further, only a small portion of those glassworkers married in the decade 1896–1905, who had been born in the Tarn, were themselves sons of glassworkers. Only 8 of 118, or about 6 percent, of this group belonged to glassworker families that had migrated to and settled in Carmaux.[5]

This shift in their place of origin was not the only change in Carmaux's glassworker population. Most of the workers who replaced those who departed for Albi (and other towns) after the strike were new to the craft of bottle blowing. Despite the fact that many of his most skilled souffleurs had quit the Verrerie Sainte Clothilde, Rességuier had little difficulty training the new recruits. Tasks were simple enough for gamins or even porteurs to perform. Experienced craftsmen complained that the apprenticeship system had become "completely fouled up." Positions were leveled and skilled workers no longer had "the right to prevent a gamin or a porteur" from blowing a bottle.[6] In 1900, furthermore, whatever skill had been required of a glassworker was superseded by the introduction of the Boucher blowing machine. With three or four days of training anyone could produce a perfect bottle. "Workers are seated in front of a machine, far from the furnaces, and their work consists of opening and closing molds by pressing [certain] pedals . . . the work requires no skill and causes no fatigue."[7]

For a number of years Rességuier used both the old and new methods of producing bottles. On October 6, 1900, only one furnace was replaced by a Boucher machine and many of the skilled glassworkers who had been displaced were hired by a firm in Brazil.[8] By 1906, though some skilled workers were still employed, the distinctions among glassblowers and between glassblowers and auxiliary workers at the factory had become less and less clear. Machine operators appear to have had status almost equivalent to that of the verriers, since, though they lacked the artisan's skills, they nonetheless performed the same functions as the souffleur and his assistant. And there were no distinctions in wages—souffleurs and machine operators earned about eight francs a day in 1906. The changing usage in official sources of terms originally denoting precise tasks mirrored these occupational changes. Police and census records alternately designated the same man as a gamin and as a *manoeuvre* (common laborer), and the term *ouvrier verrier*, originally reserved for the glassblowers, was now applied to anyone in Rességuier's employ.[9]

The changes that took place at Carmaux occurred as well at Albi, though rather more slowly and with somewhat different manifestations. The Verrerie Ouvrière d'Albi, with the motto of Fourier, "Capital, Travail, Talent," emblazoned on its walls, began production at the end of 1896. The buildings and furnaces were built by some 200 glassworkers from Carmaux and other dedicated militants who left more lucrative jobs to construct the cooperative.

For a number of years the Verrerie Ouvrière faltered, operating at a deficit and paying barely anything to its employees. Glassworkers who had earned as much as 230 francs a month at Carmaux in 1895 earned as little as 50–100 francs a month in 1897 and 1898 Albi. In addition, 20–40 percent was deducted from each man's pay to help fund the operations of the plant.[10] As a result, the poverty of the glassworkers in Albi was well known and often remarked upon in the city. Glassworkers' wives and daughters became frequent visitors to the convent in Albi which distributed food to the poor. The nuns referred to them always as "the aristocrats," remarking on their dignity and pride.[11]

In these early years the workforce consisted primarily of

the former union glassworkers from Carmaux. Dedicated to
the idea of the cooperative, many were willing to undergo
temporary hardship in order to prove the feasibility of
"association." Most were skilled craftsmen who had fought
to preserve the status of their skill at Carmaux or elsewhere.
They were satisfied with the fact that work was organized
traditionally at the Verrerie Ouvrière. Teams of souffleurs,
gamins and grands garçons blew bottles in two eight-hour
shifts.[12] But hardship and political differences among the
cooperators drove many early enthusiasts from Albi by
1897. Many of those who anticipated that things would be
better than before found themselves "far from the hopes
we envisioned" and they refused to endure severe economic
hardship in the name of an uncertain long-range security.[13]
The number of employees dropped from 240 to 150 by

5. Glassworkers building the Verrerie Ouvrière, Albi, 1896.

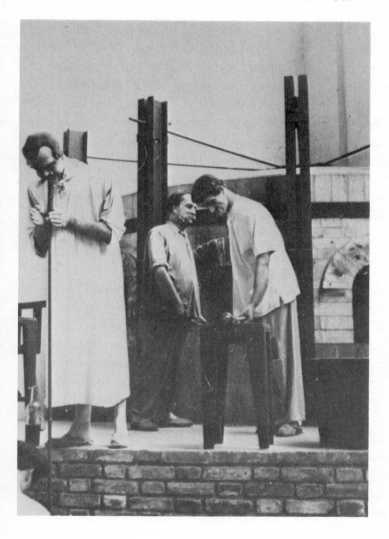

6. Wax models of an *équipe* of glassworkers in 1896, at the Musée de la Verrerie Ouvrière, Albi.

early 1898.[14] By November, 1898, there were again 240
workers. The new additions, however, were very different
from the craftsmen they replaced. They were recruited
from among the same groups to whom Rességuier had
turned after the 1895 strike at the Verrerie Sainte Clothilde.

The regulations for the factory at Albi were more severe
than Rességuier's ever had been. In part, this was a result
of the extreme pressure under which the cooperators
labored; they could not afford to indulge the luxuries of
skilled artisans. In addition, the administrators had to deal
with a number of anarchists who wanted the factory to be
a place in which workers enjoyed complete freedom, to
work or not to work, to fulfill themselves as they chose.
But the rules were also addressed to a new kind of worker,
one who had not experienced factory routine or the discipline of this particular kind of work. Aimed at enforcing
the principles of "community, solidarity, and political
liberty which ought to guide socialists," they were also an
attempt to introduce workers into the discipline required
by work in a factory. Drunkenness, quarrels, and distur-
bances were prohibited. Theft of tools and materials
brought immediate dismissal. Lateness was punished and
unexcused absence was not tolerated; even insults to
superiors brought the possibility of loss of one's job.[15]
Drawn up by the same men who had written the union
statutes of 1892, the work rules of the Verrerie Ouvrière
were remarkable for the absence of any references to craft
relationships, to rules of promotion, or to the training of
apprentices. These may have been mentioned in the union
statutes. But since the union and the administration were
the same body, the emphasis on discipline and conduct and
the exclusion of any reference to apprenticeship indicate a

change in the kind of work performed and in the experience and origins of the workers.

Glassmaking was no longer an exclusive craft by 1900. In
fact, there was little to distinguish it from many other
semiskilled trades. Glassworkers' wages remained high compared to other workers' wages in Carmaux, but the differences were not nearly so great as in earlier years. In
1882 a glassworker earned twelve francs a day, over three
times as much as the highest paid miner. Even apprentices
at the glassworks enjoyed more material prosperity than
miners, earning an average daily wage of four or five
francs.[16] During the first decade of the twentieth century,
however, a glassworker brought home less than one and
one-half times as much money as a miner. And the highest
paid miners earned more than most grands garçons.[17]

Although glassmaking did not pay as well as it had in the
past, it still represented an improvement for those just
entering the trade. For many of them the departure of the

Table 19. Average Daily Wages of Glassworkers and Miners in
Carmaux, 1902 and 1906 (Francs, Centimes)

Glassworkers	Wages	Miners (1902)	Wages
Souffleur	8.00	Piqueur, mineur, boiseur	5.45
Grand garçon	4.50	Aide	4.45–4.95
Gamin	2.60	Rouleur	2.50
Machine operators[a]	8.00		

Sources: For glassworkers: A.D. Tarn, IV M 2 95. (Wages at Albi were one or
two francs higher in each category, in part because the Boucher automatic
blower had not been introduced. A.D. Tarn, IV M 2 97.) For miners:
Trempé, *Les Mineurs de Carmaux,* 337.
[a]Operated the automatic blower.

more skilled to factories as yet unmechanized, or to other
jobs, opened hitherto closed positions. A glassworker still
earned considerably more than a miner and, as the cost of
living soared between 1900 and 1914, many young men
sought the material advantages glassmaking offered.[18]
Satisfaction with their upward occupational mobility made
a new glassworkers' union unnecessary. In addition, the
availability of better jobs drew dissatisfied young miners
from the mines, thereby depriving the miners' union of its
most discontented and most militant constituents.

Having attempted to improve conditions for wagon
rollers and aides in the mines with militant union action,
and having succeeded but little, the young men in those
positions began leaving the mines after 1903, causing a
critical shortage of personnel. Between 1902 and 1910, the
Campagnie des Mines registered net losses of personnel, for
young men were not entering the mines in these years
either.[19] If at all possible their fathers sent them to the
glassworks or to another city rather than to a stagnant
situation like their own, in the mines. (The difficulties of
local recruitment did not diminish and the company was
forced, after 1912, to begin hiring "strangers," miners from
other parts of France.)[20] The average age of miners continued to increase between 1900 and 1914, reflecting the
aging of personnel and the continuing inability of the
company to secure young employees. The departure of the
most dissatisfied sapped the union's strength, leaving
former militants urging aging miners resigned to their fates,
to action. Like the personnel of the mines, the union itself
"aged and was menaced by sclerosis."[21] The miners' union
nonetheless continued to exist as an organization, thanks
largely to the efforts of a few dedicated militants. In

contrast, there was no glassworkers union at all in Carmaux after 1895.

Despite repeated urgings by the militants at Albi and offers of help from the socialist miners in the town, the new glassworkers of Carmaux did not resurrect the union. There were several attempts, all thwarted by Rességuier. But the lack of a union could only be attributed partly to the strength of the Director's opposition. Even the militants placed blame elsewhere. The articles of the Albi militants addressed to their comrades at the Verrerie Sainte Clothilde blamed the glassworkers' passivity. "Ask yourself comrades," wrote Marien Baudot in 1899 "if someone has the right to make you die of shame by threatening to make you die of hunger."[22] At a special public meeting in Carmaux of the National Congress of Glassworkers (held in Albi in 1906), Victor Griffuelhes, the secretary of the Confédération Générale du Travail, and several other prominent national leaders pointed to the "shame" of Carmaux's glassworkers' failure to organize. It was the glassworkers' duty, Griffuelhes told an audience consisting overwhelmingly of miners, to "revive the memory" of the struggles of their brothers in Albi.[23]

Each time some glassworkers did attempt to form a union they were fired by Rességuier. But in any case their following was small and their dismissal occasioned no outburst by most of their fellow glassworkers. Many socialists felt that the introduction of the Boucher machine in October, 1900, would certainly revitalize the trade union among the glassworkers of Carmaux. Officials, too, were apprehensive about the effects of the impending automation. The police chief of Carmaux wrote to his counterpart in Cagnac in September inquiring as to how the glassworkers there had reacted to the Boucher machine.[24] And in Carmaux, during the week prior to the arrival of the automatic blower, a small group of employees had refused to work for several minutes and sang the "International" in apparent protest.[25] But though the Boucher machine displaced one-third of the glassworkers at the factory, few expressed opposition to the mechanization or concern for their jobs by joining a union. An organizing meeting held on October 14 drew 134 of 900 workers at the factory—hardly equivalent to the almost unanimous support that existed for the union in 1890.[26] A rally on December 24 to further the union's effort drew 600 people, most of them miners. The representatives of glassworkers were Baudot and Aucouturier of Albi.[27] In 1906, new efforts met with a similar lack of enthusiasm; only 84 glassworkers agreed to adhere to the union.[28]

The leaders of the drive to re-form a glassworkers' union in Carmaux do not appear to have been typical of their potential followers. Several had worked in Albi at the Verriere Ouvrière and were probably sent back to Carmaux to organize the workers there. Others, exemplified by Victor Teysseyre who participated in the two attempts to unionize in 1900 and 1906, were associated with a long tradition of militant action in trades other than glassblowing.[29] Teysseyre's father had been a blacksmith at the mines. In 1869, he had served as a delegate to negotiations with the mining company and he helped organize and lead the strike of that year.[30]

The few militants like Teysseyre who led the union efforts in 1900 and 1906 seem to have been more interested in organizing a union for the sake of organizing a union than in speaking directly to the problems of twentieth-century glassworkers. Nowhere does this appear

more clearly than in the statutes of 1900 of the Chambre
syndical des verriers de Carmaux. Those of 1900 almost
exactly duplicated the union statutes of 1892.[31] The 1892
provisions about the length of apprenticeship, punishments
for violating rules of training, and payments to the union
of regular fees upon promotion were hopelessly outdated
at the Verrerie Sainte Clothilde in 1900. There was no need
to regulate apprenticeship when almost all need for apprentices and even for skilled workers was disappearing. Moreover, the statutes only mentioned unemployment very
generally and never referred to the new technological
unemployment which had already hit a portion of the glassworkers at the Verrerie Sainte Clothilde. Unlike the authors
of the statutes of 1892, the organizers of 1900 and 1906
were not appealing directly to issues which glassworkers
immediately confronted. Perhaps their own long experience
in trade unions had convinced them of the efficacy of
such organizations. Perhaps, too, many were socialists who
recognized the importance of unions in creating and acti-
vating working-class consciousness. For them the union
would serve a political function. Thinking of the union
largely as an arm of the class struggle, these organizers
appealed to class solidarity more than to immediate problems. Certainly the speeches of the national union officials,
as well as those of the socialists at Albi, stressed the political aspect of a union. From 1898 to 1906 glassworkers at
the Verrerie Sainte Clothilde were called upon to serve the
"struggle" and to do their "duty [as] conscientious
workers." There were general references to glassworkers'
interests and to the futures of their children, but even
interest was defined in terms of the larger movement "of
. . . brothers in struggle and misery."[32]
    There are several possible explanations for the failure of

the new glassworker leaders to speak to the specific concerns of their potential constituency. One involves the position of the leaders themselves. In 1890, the union was led and organized by souffleurs, acting as a group and speaking to common concerns. In 1900 and 1906, the leaders held diverse positions in the factory with no single group predominating. Most of the union officials of 1900 were listed as "ouvriers verriers" (but this no longer necessarily specified a particular function), but only half seem to have been souffleurs. Information for 1906 is more specific.[33] The seven elected to official positions included two souffleurs, one grand garçon (also listed as manoeuvre), two gamins (listed as manoeuvres as well), one *ramasseur de verre*, and one machine operator.[34] They seem to have been linked more by a common ideology than by a shared sense of craft. For the most part they were apparently convinced militants, who based their appeal on their ideological beliefs and on the political needs of workers as they had already defined them. The correctness of the socialist analysis had been confirmed for them by their own (or their fathers') experience. Their outlook and their beliefs need only be articulated to become self-evident.

Another related explanation has to do with the constituency to which the leaders appealed. Unlike the souffleurs of 1892, the new glassworkers were not unified by a threat to their positions and to the craft they practiced. Rességuier's threat to fire them if they joined a union, therefore, was taken seriously. In 1890, being fired did not seem that much worse an alternative than passively accepting the destruction of the craft. But in 1900, despite the threat of unemployment from automation, being fired was far worse than continuing to hold a job which represented real eco-

New Glassworkers and Old

nomic improvement. A diverse group, from different backgrounds, with no traditional family affiliations to the craft, the new glassworkers lacked the sense of craft unity and of membership in a "corporation" that had characterized their predecessors. Even if the leaders had appealed to immediate economic and social concerns, it is by no means certain that a common denominator of interest could have been found either among themselves or among the general body of workers at the factory. Since glassmaking was no longer a craft, and the new glassworkers did not really think of themselves as craftsmen, the new workers did not have the same career expectations as their predecessors. They had not invested time or money in learning skills they expected to practice for life. And if unemployment threatened after 1900, they could seek to perform other kinds of factory labor not necessarily connected with glass bottles. For the most part, the new glassworkers defined their interest narrowly, in terms of their jobs, their wages, and the houses and gardens their savings might enable them to buy.

Although the new glassworkers at the Verrerie Sainte Clothilde never succeeded in reestablishing a union, at the Verrerie Ouvrière d'Albi the union was perhaps the most important single institution. Union membership was mandatory for all workers. In fact it was a prerequisite for employment.[35] Yet if the importance of a union in a worker's life is judged by his participation rather than by mere membership, the glassworkers at Albi appear rather more similar to their contemporaries at Carmaux than to their predecessors. At the Verrerie Ouvrière the union represented the administrators rather than rank-and-file workers.

181

Although it was a cooperative, ownership of the Verrerie Ouvrière was limited from the beginning. Five-eighths of the shares were owned by representative organizations of labor and socialism, most of which were located in Paris. Three-eighths were held by the leading militants of Carmaux in the name of the union. Moreover, the shareholders were a closed group; no new shares were issued nor were shares split among workers at the Verrerie Ouvrière. The former trade union leaders of Carmaux (Aucouturier, Baudot, Charpentier, Renoux, and Gidel) became administrators at Albi.[36] Indeed, their union activities had prepared them for this role. As union leaders, they developed organizational and administrative skills equal, if not superior, to their skills as bottle blowers. When Rességuier met his employee Aucouturier in the street or at the factory in the early 1890's, he often had asked for advice about changes he contemplated in the factory.[37] And when arbitration of disputes occurred in 1891 and 1895, the leaders sat side by side with representatives of their employer, with lawyers and members of Parliament.[38] Collection and distribution of strike funds involved deftness in economics as well as in organizing. And the planning and carrying out of a strike demanded efficiency and skill.

The process of seeking protection of their jobs through the union led to unforeseen consequences for the leadership. It created the potential for new careers as directors and administrators of unions and other workers' organizations. In an earlier period, master craftsmen often became the owners of small glass works. Although this practice ended early in the nineteenth century, as late as 1875 several owners of glassworks boasted of their ability to match the skill of their best souffleur.[39] More frequently,

glassworkers advanced to clerical or to administrative
positions, from blue-collar skilled jobs to white-collar posts
as accountants, bookkeepers, and sales representatives for
the glass factory.[40] In the 1890's advances of both kinds
were all but impossible. The separation between owners
and workers, between capital and labor was far too great.
Few workers could hope to amass the capital now required
to build a large glassworks. (The initial capital for the
Verrerie Ouvrière was 500,000 francs in 1896.) In addition,
the larger numbers of workers at any particular plant and
recruitment of white-collar workers outside the factory,
among different groups in the population, prevented all but
a select few glassworkers from becoming accountants,
salesmen, or managers. Yet, interestingly, unions allowed
their officials to develop administrative abilities like those
once developed by a master craftsman. These abilities
enabled them to achieve an advance similar to that of their
most favored predecessors. The skills they learned as heads
of the Chambre syndical des verriers de Carmaux enabled
them to become the directors of their own cooperative
glass factory, the Verrerie Ouvrière d'Albi.

For several years the eight administrators served as glassblowers as well as managers. Only the worker-director and
the bookkeeper held full-time positions. The other six
worker-administrators fulfilled administrative functions
part-time and blew bottles for the remainder of the day.[41]
Yet, despite their participation in the routine work of the
factory, the administrators were a distinctly separate group
at the Verrerie Ouvrière. Aucouturier, Renard, Baudot,
Charpentier, Gervier, Gidel, and Renoux continued as
union officers while they directed the glassworks. But
their concern with economic success and their daily pre-

occupations with administrative problems widened the gap between them and the men who worked under their direction. Increasingly, the experience of the leaders of the cooperative diverged from that of full-time souffleurs. There had always been social distinctions between leaders and followers even in Carmaux. But after 1896, these were reinforced by definable occupational differences as the militants followed a path parallel to the one taken by only a few fortunate and well-placed souffleurs in the early nineteenth century. By 1909, the Verrerie Ouvrière had opened sales offices in several cities. These were manned by the former union organizers of 1890. Aucouturier was at Toulouse; Gidel lived in Bordeaux; and Baudot was at the cooperative's headquarters in Paris. Renoux and Jean Boyanique were traveling salesmen stationed at Toulouse and Paris, respectively.[42]

The former leaders of 1895, once Rességuier's most highly skilled craftsmen, were now managers of a prospering factory, practicing the skills of business administrators and, despite their continued socialist and union affiliations, moving in a new social milieu. Officers of socialist and trade union organizations, like managers of cooperatives, no longer performed manual labor. Their style of life and work experience removed them from their own manual labor origins and from the factory experiences of the workers they represented. Yet they retained absolute control and direction of the union, and no new leaders emerged between 1896 and 1909. In 1907 Auguste Sallès who had been president of the union in Carmaux in 1894 was president of the Chambre syndicale des ouvriers verriers et similaires d'Albi.[43] The names of union officials and of administrators were the same. The retention of leadership by the leading militants from Carmaux was evidence of the separation between the union leadership and membership, between administrators and workers at the Verrerie Ouvrière. When Louis Renoux resigned an administrative post in 1898, a leading glassworker socialist from Cambrai, came to replace him. He was hired originally as a grand garçon, despite protests from employees that no more workers were needed. But he was brought, nonetheless, since it was felt that his political position as an active socialist and his trade union experience better equipped him as a director than any of the rank-and-file glassworkers already in the factory.[44]

The protests of workers in the factory, frequently led by anarchists who opposed everything the socialists stood for, reflected the division that had occurred. In 1897, four workers were fired from the Verrerie Ouvrière for breaking the rules of work. They blamed the administration for every difficulty that existed and though their attack was colored by their bitterness and ideological enmity, it nonetheless offers insight into the operations of the cooperative.[45] The dissidents blamed the poverty they experienced during 1896 on the administrators who "ordered everything, bought all materials and spent all the money without ever consulting or accounting for their actions to the glassworkers."[46] Rules also were said to be enforced inconsistently. Though they were glassblowers too, the directors were never punished for latenesses or absences. In addition, instead of constructing additional furnaces to employ more workers, the directors had built an office building "resembling a castle."[47] Indeed, the office became a symbol of the separation between the directors and the glassworkers. Moreover, the separation was perceived by outsiders as well.

In awarding damages to four workers who sued the Verrerie Ouvrière in 1897, the Justice of the Peace at Albi presented a hostile but nevertheless revealing argument. He maintained that if the dispute had been one between real employers and their employees he would have acted differently. But since "workers must never be superior to other workers even if they are called administrators," he ruled that the administrators had acted illegally by firing the four.[48] In fact the administrators increasingly acted less like workers and more like business managers. At a congress of glassworkers in 1903, the directors of the Verrerie Ouvrière as heads of the union officially represented the glassworkers of Albi. Yet, they refused to adhere to the newly formed federation unless it exempted the Verrerie Ouvrière from complying with other unions' demands for the regulation of production and the breaking of rejects. Although practices at the Albi glassworks violated the federation's program, Renoux and Boyanique justified the exceptionalism of their establishment. "Since only the proletariat is our employer, we do not think we will ever have to resort to strike."[49] Business success, they argued, demanded efficiency and expertise and in any case, since they were the heads of the union, the directors of the cooperative represented the glassworkers employed there.

Since no rank-and-file workers were active in the union it is difficult to assume that Renoux and Boyanique reflected much more than their own sentiments, those of men concerned with running a successful business (albeit one organized on cooperative principles). Their patronizing references to the glassworkers they directed were yet another indication of their distance from the rank and file.

Boyanique proudly told the congress how the militants' example "raised the moral level of the glassworkers of Albi."[50] However valid the economic and political considerations upon which they based their actions, the administrators appear to have used the union to impose their will from above, rather than as a reflection of the ideas and outlook of those below.

Yet after some initial bitterness inspired and led by anarchists, opposed as much to the ideology as to the practice of the administrators, there was little protest by the employees at the Verrerie Ouvrière against their employers. By 1900, the Verrerie Ouvrière had begun to realize a profit and by 1901 its workers earned what Rességuier's workers did. Whatever their origins, most glassworkers at the Verrerie Ouvrière seem to have preferred the continued economic success of the factory to a struggle with the administration for control of the union.

* * * * *

The glassworkers of the late 1890's thus differed markedly from their predecessors. For the most part they were new men indifferent to the issues underlying the militant trade unionism of 1890–1895. But even the old craftsmen who had led the struggles of those years changed with the times. The union had failed to save the craft, but as bottle blowing demanded less skill, many skilled craftsmen managed to find positions at glassworks which had not yet mechanized. Thus, when the Boucher machine arrived at Carmaux, many souffleurs and their apprentices sought employment at Albi. Some even moved as far away as Brazil. In addition, a glassblower's working life was relatively short. By age forty or forty-five most were unable to continue practicing their craft.[51] Since mechanization did not occur simultaneously at every glassworks in France, the final stages of transition from craft to semiskilled labor occurred gradually. The few remaining craftsmen adapted their own lives by moving to centers where bottles still were blown by hand. Most gave up the union as a means of dealing with changes in the craft.

After 1895 union membership dropped sharply. In that year too, the Fédération du Verre disbanded. *Le Reveil des Verriers* struggled against the inevitable for four more years and finally suspended publication on July 30, 1899.[52] The Federation attributed some of its difficulties to the drain on its resources of the strikes of 1894 and 1895 at Rive-de-Gier and Carmaux. The necessity of supporting both strikes diverted other glassworkers from dealing with local issues and it made membership in the national body a costly proposition which offered but little remuneration in terms of successful or even possible collective local action. Yet loss of interest in union was the primary difficulty the Federation faced. Appeals for funds had "fallen on deaf ears" and the largest section of the Federation, consisting of those who blew ordinary dark wine bottles (*verre-noir*), had abandoned the union "almost entirely."[53] Carmaux, once a leader of "verre-noir" had become a "hot-bed of renegades."[54]

Even those who continued as active trade unionists modified their aims after 1900. In 1902 a group of glassworkers from the North formed a new national federation under the aegis of the Confédération Générale du Travail.[55] Most affiliates came from the nonmechanized glass houses. Faced nonetheless with imminent extinction of their craft their concerns were decidedly different from those of the glassworkers of the 1890's, who also had faced major alterations in their craft. The resolutions of the Congresses of 1902, 1903, and 1906 dealt with protecting the health and moral life of individual workers. The militancy of the souffleurs of the 90's was gone, replaced by a yearning for security on the part of aging craftsmen. "Yes, to satisfy hunger and to enjoy some comfort, to learn and to teach others in order to struggle against moral and physical degeneration . . . That is the whole question!"[56] Resolutions dealt with the uncertainty of continued employment and with low wages in terms of a worker's health and security. The problem of alcoholism was treated as seriously as the introduction of automatic blowing machines. References to the craft were gone, replaced by discussion of the lot of the individual worker and the future of the class. And strikes and even arbitration were barely mentioned as a means of redressing grievances.

At the congress of 1903 a unanimous resolution called for a study of mechanization by all member unions, to insure that "the machine, a product of science, functions to everyone's advantage and not only for the profit of a few."[57] The vagueness and the brevity of this proposition indicate the paucity of means to deal with the problem glassworkers felt they faced.

In 1906, the delegates finally worked out a program specifically addressed to the problem of "overproduction." The resolution is worth quoting at length:

The Congress, considering that each year . . . [new] machinery augments production [of glass] in considerable proportions; considering . . . that work in hot weather constitutes a danger to the health of glassworkers and is a cause of social degeneration . . . considering, finally, that the worker has many expenses, and that often, in spite of himself, he is forced to seek a purely illusory strength in alcoholic beverages . . . the effect of which . . . makes him a weak being with no will . . . [aggravating] his tuberculosis, so easy to contract in our industry, also leading him to worse moral degradation.

For these reasons, the Congress demands that employers set a date and a place in order to discuss [with us] this grave question.[58]

The problems facing these glassworkers were now open to negotiation. In fact, the resolution sounded more like an appeal to employers than a demand that they comply. Phrases like moral and social "degradation" were calculated to arouse concern on the part of employers and not fear of a strike or some other militant collective action. The Federation of the 1890's had called upon glassworkers themselves to withhold their skills or to exercise political pressure through their unions; the Federation of the early 1900's, although it urged workers to "organize" in order to "make tomorrow . . . [less] doubtful,"[59] also asked employers to aid their efforts. In fact, the burden of ameliorating the glassworkers' lot appeared to rest less with themselves, than with the men for whom they worked.[60]

And if their employers did not care for them, perhaps the burdens of old age would be lightened by their sons. If the evidence from Carmaux and Albi is at all typical it indicates that the old glassworkers did not send their sons into glass factories but to school and into nonmanual while-collar jobs available in the expanding bureaucracies of cities.[61] Almost every child of the militant glassworkers who founded the Verrerie Ouvrière left not only glassmaking but all manual labor occupations. Although many retained their fathers' socialist loyalties, they became teachers, civil servants, or white-collar workers in the growing Bureaucracies of Carmaux and Albi. Typical were Louis Renoux's daughter, who became a teacher, and his son, who became a postal clerk.

The militancy of the glassworkers of Carmaux between 1890 and 1895 thus represented the last stand of artisans in the face of mechanization. Given the turnover in the glassmaking population, it would be misleading to say that the old artisans ended by accepting the deflation of their status and the destruction of their craft. In one sense, of course, they did. No amount of striking and organization had prevented the consequences of technological innovation. Yet, though the union failed to achieve its goal, most artisans did not enter the new factories. Some managed to find jobs at unmechanized factories which still required their skills, and some forged new and better-paying careers. Even those who stayed on despite the demeaning of their skills and the diminishing of their wages did not pass their misfortune on to their sons. Instead, the old artisans were replaced in the factories by newcomers to the trade who considered themselves fortunate to acquire the few skills needed by a twentieth-century glassworker. The decline of militancy thus coincided with the arrival of a new kind of worker for whom technological developments had created opportunities for greater material prosperity. The new glassworkers and their successors would later participate in a resurgence of militant trade union activity. But that is a story quite different from the one we have told. It is a story of the experiences and grievances of twentieth-century glassworkers who formed unions in the context of their own times and not as the inevitable consequence of the activities of their predecessors.

The "corporation" of artisan glassblowers disappeared as the nineteenth century ended. There are, of course, still men in France today who can blow a perfect bottle. They sometimes are called upon to perform specialized tasks for large bottle factories. In Albi, at the Verrerie Ouvrière (which still is a cooperative though it operates on contract to Saint Gobain, which has a near monopoly on bottle production in France), an old man comes once a week to blow *bonnebonnes*, the very large bottles which are as decorative as they are practical. But he is a man of the past and even more significant, he is considered and considers himself an artist. He does not identify with the glass-workers around him for he cannot operate a machine and they look upon him (not without a certain nostalgia) as a remarkable, if impractical, antique. If the glassworkers at Albi today still nourish the tradition of 1895 and associate the strike and the founding of their cooperative with a militant tradition among glassworkers, they nonetheless have translated that tradition into modern terms. They would be surprised to learn that the militancy of their predecessors involved an attempt to defend a highly skilled, exclusive craft against the inroads of mechanization. And they would be even more dismayed to discover that those militant artisans ultimately left the craft and discouraged their children from entering it. There is no direct link between the new glassworkers and the old. The identical-ness of occupational title masks two vastly different experi-ences, that of the modern factory worker and of the nineteenth-century artisan, whose skill and corporate identity are now obsolete.

Epilogue
Three Portraits

These portraits illustrate three phases in the history of the glassworkers of Carmaux. Each is drawn from a different generation, each represents a different occupational and social experience. The lives of the three men recapitulate in miniature the history of the glassworkers of Carmaux.

Jean-Baptiste Auguste Alary

Jean-Baptiste Alary was born in 1844 at Blaye, the commune bordering on Carmaux and the site of the Solages's château where the Verrerie Royale was housed. He grew up in a family of glassworkers and at an early age began to learn the craft of his father. But, unlike many of the glassworkers of his age, Alary belonged to a family with deep roots in Carmaux. Indeed, Alary's grandfather, father, and brothers were all born and died in Blaye. In addition, each generation augmented the family landholdings and in turn passed them on to its children.

Alary's great-grandfather, apparently the first member of the family employed at the glass house, worked in the warehouses in 1812.[1] His son, Jean-Pierre, who was Jean-

Baptiste's grandfather, was noted on the company records
in 1816 as Alary, *fils*, stoker.[2] Among the best-paid of
auxiliary workers, stokers regulated the temperature of the
furnaces. In fact, the master stoker also "supervised all
activities in the shop when the director was temporarily
absent."[3]

By 1835 the elder Alary had retired. Company records
listed him as Alary, *grand-père*, pensioner. He must have
died shortly after 1835 for his wife shows up as a pensioner
in the 1838 records and then, in 1840, as the "supervisor
of maintenance and laundries of the enterprise."[4] Dedicated employees and their wives were often guaranteed an
income after retirement by the paternalistic Solages family.

In 1835, Jean-Pierre Alary's designation had been
changed from fils to père, his title from stoker to master
stoker. He had reached the top of the hierarchy of auxiliaries. His son could improve upon his economic and occupational positions only by becoming a glassblower. That, in
fact, was precisely what he did. In 1835, Jean-Pierre Salvy
Alary, listed as Alary, fils, began work as a gamin. The
tenure and dedication of his father and grandfather won
entry into the corporation of glassworkers for a member of
the third generation of their family. Jean-Pierre Salvy also
inherited the land his grandfather and father had owned.
Moreover, before he completed his apprenticeship he
married the daughter of a farmer, whose inheritance enlarged his own. By the time of the birth of his youngest
son, Jean-Baptiste, in 1844, he listed two occupations for
himself: glassworker and farmer.[5]

Jean-Baptiste grew up in a more rural setting then most
of his fellow glassworkers. The entire family cultivated the
land and the men were also practiced artisans. Although

the glassworks was moved from the Solages's château to the site of the railway station in 1861, Jean-Pierre Salvy and his two sons, Jean Salvy and Jean-Baptiste, continued to work as glassblowers. Jean Salvy married in 1865; Jean-Baptiste wed the daughter of a coachman in 1869. Their older sister, Rosalie, married glassworker Paul Marion.[6] By 1890, Jean-Baptiste Alary and Paul Marion, both established souffleurs, were the two largest glassworker landowners in Carmaux.

All three of Jean-Pierre Salvy's offspring owned and lived in their own houses. And none lived in the glassworkers' quarter surrounding the Verrerie Sainte Clothilde. Unlike their father, Jean-Pierre and Jean-Baptiste had large families. Three of Jean-Pierre's six children reached adulthood; and seven of Jean-Baptiste's nine attained maturity and married in Carmaux. The sons of both men were apprenticed to their fathers and, like them, became glassworkers.

Jean-Pierre Salvy died in 1883, but he lived to see his oldest son further the family's achievement. After some years as a glassblower, his namesake Jean-Pierre was rewarded for his and his family's dedicated service at the glassworks of Carmaux. He was promoted to a white-collar job as keeper of the books at the warehouse.[7]

Jean-Baptiste was not promoted. But although he continued as a glassblower at the factory he also began to engage in the politics of the city. In 1881, he was the only worker on a municipal council consisting of landowners and small shopkeepers. Undoubtedly he qualified for the seat because of his landholdings. He was still in office in 1884 and apparently held his seat until the socialist victory in 1892.[8]

Epilogue

In 1896, another Alary contested a municipal election. This was Jean-Baptiste Emile (referred to simply as Baptiste), the son of Jean-Baptiste. Born in 1873, Baptiste learned his father's craft, married a miner's daughter, and settled in Carmaux.[9] He was hostile to the union and, though forced to join it or relinquish his job in 1891, he was noted for his reluctance to pay dues or to attend meetings. He told a union delegate to "drop dead" in 1894 and was threatened with expulsion more than once.[10] He never lost his job, however. Baptiste refused to strike during the strike of 1895, and he appeared as one of six hostile witnesses at the trial of Michel Aucouturier.[11] After the strike, in May, 1896, he ran for the municipal council of Carmaux on the Solages's backed Républicain-Progressiste list, but he was defeated by the socialists.[12] At Blaye, however, his cousin, Jean Marion, who also ran on the "antirevolutionary," antisocialist list, was triumphant.[13]

The Alary family's experience at the glassworks in Carmaux spanned a century. From 1800 to 1900 its sons prospered from their affiliations with the glassworks. Following a traditional but rapidly disappearing path, Alarys had advanced from skilled auxiliaries to glassblowers to white-collar employees. Son succeeded father from one generation to the next. Unlike most of their fellow glassworkers the Alarys never left the town of their birth. Unlike the semipeasant miners of Carmaux, they were relatively large and prosperous landowners. Their land and their tenure in Carmaux brought them local and political prominence, which, however, differed dramatically from the prominence of socialist political figures like Michel Aucouturier. The Alarys not only refused to follow the socialist programs of the 1890's, but they actively opposed them. However much the conditions of work at the Verrerie Sainte Clothilde might have changed, the Alarys continued as dedicated and loyal employees, resisting unionization and the socialist politics of their fellow workers.

Michel Aucouturier

Unlike Jean-Baptiste Alary whose name can be found in the usual number of civil acts, more prominently than most in land records, and only rarely in police archives, Michel Aucouturier's police dossiers were far bulkier than any other official records concerning him. Although Alary represented the fourth generation of his family's service to the glassworks at Carmaux, Aucouturier was the first of his family to work there. And unlike Alary who saw his sons become the fifth generation of the family to enter the craft of glassblowing at Carmaux, Aucouturier was fired after only a few years of employment. If the Alarys' occupational pattern was more traditional than Aucouturier's, Aucouturier's experience (though unusual because of his positions of leadership) was nonetheless more typical of glassworkers in the 1890's.

Michel Aucouturier was born in Montluçon (Allier) in 1863. The oldest son of a glassworker, he followed the practice of the craft and began his apprenticeship as soon as he was old enough. Aucouturier became a souffleur around 1885, exactly the point at which technological innovations were introduced at a number of French glasshouses. Apparently, he became a militant early in his career. In 1888 he was fired during a strike of glassworkers at Montluçon and then was recruited by Rességuier to Carmaux.

When Aucouturier came to Carmaux he brought his entire family with him. The move appears to have been the first for the family in Michel's lifetime. His father and brother, both glassworkers, also found employment at the Verrerie Sainte Clothilde. The family, like most of Carmaux's glassworking families, lived together in a rented apartment on the Rue de la Verrerie, close to the factory.[14]

Soon after his arrival, Aucouturier joined with a small group of glassworkers and formed the Chambre syndicale des verriers de Carmaux. He also joined the central revolutionary committee and was judged by police to be "the most dangerous of this party." "Uncompromising on political matters," he was said to be surpassed only by his wife "who is more fanatic than he."[15] Herself a native of Montluçon, Felicie Denizot was the daughter of a blacksmith (employed at a glassworks). Aucouturier married her in Carmaux in 1890.[16]

An official of the glassworkers' union, Aucouturier was elected a municipal councillor in January 1892.[17] He served until the strike of 1895. In November, 1894, Aucouturier became Carmaux's correspondent for *La Dépêche de Toulouse*. A Guesdist, Aucouturier had differences with many of his fellow workers in the Cercle d'Etudes Sociales of Carmaux. Calvignac, for example, remembered him as "enfiefed to a party to which I do not belong." When initially the leaders of the glassworkers and the miners differed over whether to support the parliamentary candidacy of Jaurès in 1892, Aucouturier preferred an avowed socialist like Duc-Quercy. Eventually, however, he agreed to Jaurès.[18]

He was arrested at Albi in 1893 for shouting "Vive Baudin" during the visit of a state official.[19] One of the leaders of the strike of 1895, he was condemned to four months in prison for interfering with "liberté du travail." Among the most prominent of the leaders of the glass-workers in Carmaux, Aucouturier regularly attended congresses of the National Federation of glassworkers and of the Bourses du Travail. He was a founder of the Verrerie Ouvrière d'Albi and administrator of the cooperative in 1897. In 1909 he became the head of its Toulouse office.[20] Aucouturier lived at Toulouse and remained active in socialist politics until his death in 1916.

Aucouturier's daughter, Michelle, profited from her father's new occupation. She had been born in Carmaux early in 1896.[21] She was raised at the Verrerie Ouvrière and then in Toulouse among the trade union and socialist leaders who were her father's associates. Whereas daughters of glassworkers once married glassworkers, Michelle Aucouturier did not. Instead she chose someone close to what her father had become. In 1913 she married Jules Vincent Auriol, then one of the leading young socialists of the region, who was to become the first president of the Fourth Republic.

Emile Augustin Albar

Emile Albar, the son of a miner, was born in Carmaux in 1881. At the time of the strike of 1895 he was a porteur at the Verrerie Sainte Clothilde. He left work with the others for a time, but returned when the strike was settled.[22] His brother, three years his junior, joined him at the factory in 1897 or 1898. Emile married the daughter of a cultivator in 1906. His brother wed a miner's daughter a year later.[23] Neither Albar was involved in the two short-lived attempts to form a union in Carmaux after 1900. Neither seems to have been drawn to the miner-led socialist politics of the town. Both brothers enjoyed a better financial position than had their father, though neither bought land or a house, as did many of their contemporaries.

Emile Albar was the first member of his family to enter the glass factory. He may have served as a porteur for a time in the équipe headed by Baptiste Alary, the last member of his family to blow bottles in Carmaux; for, in 1896, old and new glassworkers still worked side by side. By 1914, however, the Alarys and Aucouturiers were gone. Emile Albar remained as the typical glassworker of Carmaux.

Appendix
Bibliography
Notes
Index

Abbreviations

A.D.	Archives Départementales
A.D. Tarn	Archives Départementales du Tarn
A.M.	Archives Municipales
A.N.	Archives Nationales (Paris)
A.R.	Archives Renoux (privately held by the family)
A.S.	Archives Solages (held at A.D. Tarn)
B.N.	Bibliothèque Nationale (Paris)
M.S.	Musée Social (Paris)

Table A. Occupations of Fathers of Glassworkers Married in Carmaux, by Decade, 1866–1905 (Percentages)

Years	Glass-worker	Auxiliary at glass-works	Miner	Peasant	Other[a]	Unknown	Total number of glassworker marriages
1866–1875[b]	11	3	22	11	33	19	27
1876–1885	40	5	7	9	7	33	43
1886–1895	21	8	12	13	27	19	90
1896–1905	13	4	14	18	17	34	118

Source: A.M. Carmaux, Actes de Mariages, 1866–1905.
[a] Includes small craftsmen, common laborers, and an occasional small merchant.
[b] Period of expansion. Rességuier recruits locally.

Table B. Birthplace of Glassworkers Married in Carmaux, by Decade, 1866–1905 (Percentages)

Years	Tarn	Departments contiguous to the Tarn[a]	Loire & Rhône	Other	Foreign	Total number
1866–1875	40	26	30	4	0	27
1876–1885	9	9	37[b]	44	0	43
1886–1895	18	18	12	48	2	90
1896–1905	61	14	11	14	0	118

Source: A.M. Carmaux, Actes de Mariages, 1866–1905.

[a] Departments contiguous or close enough to Carmaux, from which there may have been "normal" regional migration: Aveyron, Tarn-et-Garonne, Haute Garonne, Ariège, Gers, Lot, Herault, Gard, Lozère, Vaucluse, Aude.

[b] Glassworkers displaced by mechanization and consolidation at Rive-de-Gier and Givors.

Table C. Occupations of Fathers of Glassworkers Aged 10–19 Years, 1876, 1891, and 1896 (Percentages)

Year	Glassworker	Miner	Peasant	Other	Unknown	Total number glassworkers, ages 10–19
1876[a]	55	14	0	13	18	22
1891	17	25	6	28	23	183
1896	23[b]	26	5	27	18	151

Source: A.M. Carmaux, Liste nominative de population, 1876, 1891, 1896.

[a]It was impossible to use figures from the census of 1866. There were eleven cases, of which six provided no information, since the boys lived with widowed mothers.

[b]This increase represents a new situation rather than a reversion to 1876. Sons of "new" glassworkers may be beginning to follow their fathers' occupations. The increase also may represent only a temporary situation, in which new and old glassworkers' sons temporarily fill the places of those fired during the strike of 1895.

Appendix

Table D. Geographic Mobility of Glassworkers of Carmaux, by
Decade, 1866–1895

Years	Arrived[a] within the decade	Died in Carmaux within the decade	Departed[b] by the last year of the decade	Departures (percent)
1866–1875	105	4	69	65
1876–1885	234	7	153	65
1886–1895	465	19	199	42

Source: Family reconstitution.

[a]Arrived means first mentioned as a glassworker. Correlation with birthplace
and other information ruled out previous occupation in Carmaux in most
cases. This information, in addition to what is known about the nature of
occupational training, makes it fairly certain that geographic mobility is
being measured.

[b]Departed means not mentioned again as a glassworker and, for most cases,
name not mentioned in any civil acts under other occupations.

Bibliography

Primary Sources

I. Archives
   A. Archives Nationales
     1. BB Versements du Ministre de la Justice
       BB 18—Correspondance générale de la Division Criminelle
       BB 30—Versements de 1904, 1905, 1908, 1929, 1933, 1936, 1941, 1943, 1944
     2. C—Procès-verbaux des assemblées nationales
     3. F—Administration générale de la France
       F 1 C III—Esprit public et élections (série départementale)
       F 7—Police Générale
       F 12—Commerce et industrie
   B. Archives Départementales du Tarn (Albi)
     1. Archives de Solages
     2. Series M—Personnel, police et administration générale
     3. Series T—Instruction publique
     4. Series U—Jugements correctionnels
     5. Transcriptions d'Albi (Conservation des Hypothèques d'Albi)
   C. Archives Municipales de Carmaux
     1. Registre de la paroisse de Cramaux (sic), 1712–1789
     2. Etat Civil—Actes de Mariages, Naissances, Décès, 1853–1912

3. Liste nominative de dénombrement de population, 1851, 1856, 1861, 1866, 1872, 1876, 1881, 1886, 1891, 1896, 1901
4. Matrices Cadastrale
D. Archives Municipales de Blaye
  1. Etat Civil, 1853–1912
  2. Liste nominative de dénombrement de population, 1861, 1866, 1901
  3. Matrices cadastrale
E. Archives Municipales d'Albi
  1. Liste nominative de dénombrement de population, 1896, 1901
  2. Etat Civil, 1896–1901
F. Archives du Musée Social, Paris
G. Musée de la Verrerie Ouvrière d'Albi
H. Archives Renoux. (Private papers of Louis Renoux which include papers of the Chambre syndicale des verriers de Carmaux)

II. Printed Materials
  A. Statuts de la Chambre syndicale des verriers de Carmaux, 1891, 1892, (A.D. Tarn, Bibliothèque C 437 25 et 26)
  B. Congresses of the National Federation of Glassworkers
    1891—M.S.
    1892—B.N.
    1893—Reprinted in the March, 1894, issues of *Le Reveil des Verriers*, B.N.
    1895—Musée de la Verrerie Ouvrière, Albi
    1902—M.S.
    1903—M.S.
    1906—A.D. Tarn, IV M 2 97
  C. Direction du Travail, *Statistiques des grèves et des recours à la conciliation survenus pendant l'année*, 1893, 1895. Paris, 1894, 1896. Figures for 1890–1892 are in nos. 3 and 7 of *Notices et comptes rendus*
    Direction du Travail, *Les Associations professionnelles ouvrières*, vol. III, Paris, 1903
    Statistique générale, *Statistique annuelle du mouvement de la population 1871–1906*. Paris, 1874–1907

III. Newspapers
  Le Cri des Travailleurs, 1898–1914 (A.D. Tarn)

208

Bibliography

Journal du Tarn, 1848–1881 (intermittently) (A.D. Tarn and B.N.)

Le Républicain de Carmaux, 1889–1890 (A.D. Tarn)

Le Reveil des Verriers, 1893–1894 (B.N.); 1892–1900 (A.D. Rhône)

La Voix des Travailleurs, 1889–1898 (A.D. Tarn)

IV. Journals

Annales des Mines

Revue Historique, Littéraire et Scientifique du Tarn, 1876–1900

V. Books and Articles by Contemporaries

Anon. "The Week," *Nation*, 64 (June 3, 1897), 407.

Bernard, Edouard. *La Verité sur la Verrerie Ouvrière d'Albi*. Albi, 1913 (B.N.).

Calvignac, Jean-Baptiste. "Mémoires d'un militant mineur: J.-B. Calvignac, maire de Carmaux," présentés par R. Trempé, *Le Mouvement Social*, no. 43 (avril–juin 1963), 121–138.

Charneau, A. *Note sur les fours et appareils de verreries*. Paris, 1886 (B.N.).

Courtot, Louis, et Eugène Rey. *Rapport des délégués ouvriers de la Chambre syndicale des ouvriers réunis de Lyon*. Lyon, 1890 (B.N.).

Deffernez, Edouard. *Des Souffleurs de verre, hygiène, maladies, et accidents*. Belgium, 1880 (B.N.).

Didron, Edouard, et Clémandot. *Rapport sur les cristaux, la verrerie et les vitraux*, Exposition Universelle Internationale de 1878 à Paris, Paris, 1880.

Geugnot, E., et E. Guérard. *La Verité sur la Verrerie Ouvrière; sa création, ses résultats, par des ouvriers renvoyés*. Albi, 1897 (A.D. Tarn).

Gibon, A. *La Grève de Carmaux, de l'arbitrage légal et des conditions de l'harmonie dans l'industrie*. Paris, 1893 (B.N.).

Jaurès, Jean. *La Grève de Carmaux*. Paris, 1895.

Jolibois, E. "Les Houillères de Carmaux," *Revue Historique, Littéraire et Scientifique du Tarn*, 10 (1893), 77–90; 236–249; 330–337.

Pelletier, Pierre. *Les Verriers dans le Lyonnais et le Forez*. Paris, 1887 (B.N.).

Bibliography

Princeteau, Paul. *Les Grèves des verriers de Bordelais.* Np., 1891 (B.N.).

Rossignol, Elie A. *Monographies communales ou étude statistique, historique et monumentale du département du Tarn.* 4 vols. Toulouse, 1864–1866.

Sauzay, Alexandre. *La Verrerie depuis les temps les plus reculés jusqu'à nos jours.* Paris, 1868.

Seilhac, Léon de. *Une Enquête sociale: La grève de Carmaux et la verrerie d'Albi.* Paris, 1897.

—— *La Verrerie Ouvrière d'Albi.* Paris, 1903 (A.D. Tarn).

Talmeyr, Maurice. "Chez les verriers," *Revue des Deux Mondes,* 145 (1 Février 1898), 641–667.

Secondary Sources

I. Carmaux, Tarn, glassworkers

Armengaud, André. *Les Populations de l'Est-Aquitain au début de l'époque contemporaine.* Paris: Mouton, 1961.

—— "Coup d'état et plébiscite dans le département du Tarn," *Annales du Midi,* 64 (1952), 41–47.

Bernis, Baron G. de Pierre. *Les Mines de Carmaux, 1700–1900.* Paris, 1918 (A.D. Tarn).

Bonnet, S., C. Santini, et H. Barthélemy. "Verriers et bûcherons d'Argonne aux XVIIIe et XIXe siècles," *Le Mouvement Social,* no. 57 (1966), 143–180.

Calmels, Louis. *De Carmaux médiéval à Monestiès-Combefa et au Néo-Carmausin.* Rodez, 1932.

Dreyfus, François-Georges. "L'Industrie de la verrerie en Bas-Languedoc de Colbert à la révolution industrielle du XIXe siècle." *Annales du Midi,* 63 (1951), 43–70.

Forster, Robert. *The Nobility of Toulouse in the Eighteenth Century: A Social and Economic Study.* Baltimore: The Johns Hopkins University Press, 1960.

Goldberg, Harvey. *The Life of Jean Jaurès.* Madison: University of Wisconsin Press, 1962.

Greslé-Bouignol, M. "La Révolution de 1848 dans le Tarn," *Revue Historique et Littéraire du Languedoc,* 5 (1948), 286–299.

Luzan, A. *La Verrerie Ouvrière d'Albi.* Paris, 1922.

Mandirac, Gilbert. "Le Département du Tarn à la veille de

Bibliography

1848," *Revue Historique et Littéraire du Languedoc*, 5 (1948), 300–320.

Piganiol, Pierre. *Le Verre, son histoire, sa technique*. Paris: Hachette, 1965.

Saint-Quirnin. *Les Verriers de Languedoc, 1290–1790*. Montpellier: Extrait du Bulletin de la Société languedocienne de géographie, vols. XXVII–XXIX, 1904–1906.

Scoville, Warren C. *Revolution in Glassmaking*. Cambridge: Harvard University Press, 1948.

—— *Capitalism and French Glassmaking, 1640–1789*. Berkeley: University of California Press, 1950.

Trempé, Rolande. *Les Mineurs de Carmaux, 1848–1914*. Paris: Éditions Ouvrières, 1971.

—— "Les Ouvriers des mines de Carmaux," unpub., D.E.S., University of Toulouse, 1954.

—— "Les Premiers Luttes des mineurs de Carmaux, 1850–1883," *Cahiers Internationaux*, no. 62 (1955), 49–66.

—— "L'Echec électoral de Jaurès à Carmaux, 1898," *Cahiers Internationaux*, no. 93 (1958), 47–64.

—— "Jean-Baptiste Calvignac, 1854–1934," *Revue du Tarn*, no. 24 (décembre 1961), 399–410.

—— "Jaurès, deputé de Carmaux," in *Jean Jaurès*, edited by Vincent Auriol. Paris: Presses Universitaires de France, 1962, 86–119.

—— "Les Administrateurs des mines de Carmaux: Etude de psychologie patronale," *Le Mouvement Social*, no. 43 (avril–juin 1963), 53–92.

—— "Bibliographie française: Travaux français sur la mine et les mineurs parus depuis 1945," *Le Mouvement Social*, no. 43 (avril–juin 1963), 147–150.

—— "Jaurès et la Verrerie Ouvrière," in *Actes du Colloque Jaurès et la nation*, edited by l'Association des publications de la Faculté des Lettres et Sciences humains de Toulouse. Toulouse, 1965.

Valtax, Ludovic. *Monographie sur le mouvement de la population dans le département du Tarn de 1801 à 1911*. Albi: Imprimerie Cooperative du Sud-Ouest, 1917.

Vareilles, Jean. "Carmaux pendant la Révolution," *Revue du Tarn*, no. 40 (décembre 1965), 419–432; no. 41 (mars 1966), 69–86; no. 43 (septembre 1966), 343–349; no. 45 (mars 1967), 85–98.

Bibliography

—— "Carmaux (18 brumaire 1799 au 2 décembre 1851)," *Revue du Tarn,* no. 47 (septembre 1967), 329–348.

Viguier, H. *Evolution démographique dans le département du Tarn depuis le début du XIXe siècle.* Albi: Imprimerie des Orphelins-Apprentis, 1950.

II. The French Working-Class Movement

Aquet, J.-P. *Les Grèves sous la Monarchie de Juillet, 1830–1847.* Geneva: E. Droz, 1954.

Chatelain, Abel. "Les Migrants temporaires et la propagation des idées révolutionnaires en France au XIXe siècle," *1848: Revue des Révolutions Contemporaines,* no. 188 (mai 1951), 6–18.

Dolléans, Edouard. *Histoire du mouvement ouvrier.* 3 vols. Paris: A Colin, 1936–1953.

Duveau, Georges. *La Vie ouvrière en France sous le Second Empire.* Paris: Gallimard, 1946.

Festy, O. *Le Mouvement ouvrier au début de la Monarchie de Juillet, 1830–1834.* Paris: E. Cornely et Cie., 1908.

—— *Les Associations ouvrières encouragées par la deuxième république; documents inédits.* Paris: F. Rieder et Cie., 1915.

Goetz-Girey, R. *Le Mouvement des grèves en France, 1919–1962.* Paris: Editions Sirey, 1965.

Gossez, R. *Les Ouvriers de Paris,* vol. 24. Société d'Histoire de la Révolution de 1848, 1967.

—— "L'Organisation ouvrière à Paris sous la Seconde République," *1848: Revue des Révolutions Contemporaines,* 42 (1950), 31–45.

—— "Diversité des antagonismes sociaux vers le milieu du XIXe siècle," *Revue Economique,* no. 3 (May 1956), 439–451.

Labrousse, C.-E., ed. *Aspects de la crise et de la depression de l'économie française au milieu du XIXe siècle.* La Roche-sur-Yon: Imprimerie Centrale de l'Ouest, 1956.

Levasseur, P.E. *Histoire des classes ouvrières et de l'industrie en France de 1789 à 1870,* Paris: A. Rousseau, 1903–1904.

L'Huillier, Fernand. *La Lutte ouvrière à la fin du Second Empire.* Paris: A. Calin, 1957.

Lorwin, Val. "Working-Class Politics and Economic Development in Western Europe." *American Historical Review,* 63, no. 2 (January 1958), 338–351.

Maitron, Jean. *Dictionnaire biographique du mouvement ouvrier français.* Paris: Editions Ouvrières, 1964.

—— E. Labrousse, et al. "Le Mouvement ouvrier français dans le seconde moitié du XIXe siècle," *Le Mouvement Social.* nos. 33–34 (octobre 1960), entire issue.

Moss, B.H. "Origins of the French Labor Movement: The Socialism of Skilled Workers," unpub. diss., Columbia University, 1972.

Perrot, Michelle. "Grèves, grévistes et conjoncture. Vieux problème, travaux neufs," *Le Mouvement Social,* no. 63 (avril–juin 1968), 109–124.

Rigaudias-Weiss, Hilde. *Les Enquêtes ouvrières en France entre 1830 et 1848.* Paris: F. Alcan, 1936.

Rudé, George. *The Crowd in History.* New York: Wiley, 1964.

Tilly, Charles. "Reflections on the Revolutions of Paris," *Social Problems,* 12 (1964).

Willard, Claude. *Le Mouvement socialiste en France (1893–1905): Les Guesdistes.* Paris: Editions Sociales, 1965.

III. Demographic Studies

Annales du Demographie Historique, 1964–

Ariès, Philippe. *Histoire des populations françaises et de leurs attitudes devant la vie depuis le XVIIIe siècle.* Paris: SELF, 1948.

Barclay, George W. *Techniques of Population Analysis.* New York: Wiley, 1958

Berthier de Sauvigny, H. "Population Movements and Political Changes in Nineteenth Century France," *Review of Politics,* 19, no. 1 (January 1957), 331–347.

Biraben, J.N., M. Fleury, and L. Henry. "Inventaire par sondage des registres paroissaux de France," *Population,* 15 (1960), 25–58.

Bourgeois-Pichat, J. "Evolution de la population française depuis le XVIIIe siècle," *Population,* 6 (1951), 635–662.

Camp, Wesley D. *Marriage and the Family in France since the Revolution.* New York: Bookman Associates, 1961.

Chevalier, Louis, *La Formation de la population parisienne au XIXe siècle.* Paris: Presses Universitaires de France, 1950.

Bibliography

—— *Classes laborieuses et classes dangereuses à Paris pendant la première moitié du XIXe siècle.* Paris: Plon, 1958.

—— "Localisation industrielle et peuplement," *Population,* 1 (1946), 21–34.

Fleury, M., and L. Henry. *Des registres paroissiaux à l'histoire de la population: Manuel de dépouillement et d'exploitation de l'état civil ancien.* Paris: Institut National d'études demographiques, 1956.

—— *Nouveau Manuel de dépouillement et d'exploitation de l'état civil ancien.* Paris: Institut National d'études demographiques, 1965.

—— "Pour connaître la population de la France depuis Louis XIV. Plan de travaux par sondage," *Population,* 13 (1958), 663–686.

Gautier, E., and L. Henry, *La Population de Crulai, paroisse Normande; étude historique.* Paris: Presses Universitaires de France, 1958.

Glass, D.V., and D.E.C. Eversley, eds. *Population in History: Essays in Historical Demography.* Chicago: Aldine Publishing Company, 1965.

"Historical Population Studies," *Daedalus,* (Spring 1968), entire issue.

Pouthas, Charles. *La Population française pendant la première moitié du XIXe siècle.* Paris: Presses Universitaires de France, 1956.

Wrigley, E.A., ed. *An Introduction to English Historical Demography:* From the Sixteenth to the Nineteenth Century. New York: Basic Books, 1966.

IV. Industrialization and Working-Class Politics

Bendix, R. "The Lower Classes and the Democratic Revolution," *Industrial Relations,* 1, no. 1 (October 1961) 91–116.

—— and S.M. Lipset, *Social Mobility and Industrial Society.* Berkeley: University of California Press, 1959.

Blumer, Herbert. "Early Industrialization and the Laboring Class," *Sociological Quarterly,* 1 (January 1960), 3–14.

"Conference Report on Social Mobility," *Past and Present,* no. 32 (December 1965), 3–11.

Everitt, Alan. "Social Mobility in Early Modern England," *Past and Present,* no. 33 (April 1966), 56–73.

Bibliography

Feldman, A.S. "Economic Development and Social Mobility," *Economic Development and Cultural Change*, 8, no. 3 (April 1960), 311–321.

Friedmann, Georges. *Industrial Society*. Glencoe, Ill.: The Free Press, 1955.

Hammond, J.L. "The Industrial Revolution and Discontent," *Economic History Review*, 2 (1929–1930), 215–228.

Hobsbawm, E.J. *Labouring Men: Studies in the History of Labour*. New York: Basic Books, 1964.

Kerr, Clark, and Abraham Siegel. "The Inter-industry Propensity to Strike—An International Comparison," in *Industrial Conflict*, edited by Arthur Kornhauser et al. New York: McGraw-Hill, 1954, 189–212.

Kerr, Clark, et al. *Industrialism and Industrial Man*. Cambridge: Harvard University Press, 1960.

Leggett, John C. "Uprootedness and Working-class Consciousness," *American Journal of Sociology*. 68, no. 6 (May 1963), 682–692.

Mayer, K.M. "Social Mobility: America versus Europe," *Commentary*, 19 (April 1955), 395–396.

Miller, S.M. "Comparative Social Mobility." *Current Sociology*, 9 (1960), entire issue.

Olson, Mancur. "Rapid Economic Growth as a Destabilizing Force," *Journal of Economic History*, 23 (1963), 529–588.

Ridker, Ronald G. "Discontent and Economic Growth," *Economic Development and Cultural Change*, 11, no. 1 (October 1962), 1–15.

Rimlinger, Gaston V. "The Legitimation of Protest. A Comparative Study in Labor History." *Comparative Studies in Society and History*, 2 (1959–1960), 329–343.

Schnore, Leo F. "Social Mobility in Demographic Perspective," *American Sociological Review*, 26 (June 1961), 407–423.

Smelser, Neil. *Social Change in the Industrial Revolution*. Chicago: University of Chicago Press, 1959.

—— and S.M. Lipset, eds. *Social Structure and Mobility in Economic Development*. Chicago: Aldine Publishing Co., 1966.

Stone, Lawrence. "Social Mobility in England, 1500–1700," *Past and Present*, no. 33 (April 1966), 17–55.

Thernstrom, Stephan. *Poverty and Progress: Social Mobility in a Nineteenth Century City*. Cambridge: Harvard University Press, 1964.

—— "Working Class Social Mobility in Industrial America," in *Essays in Theory and History,* edited by Melvin Richter. Cambridge: Harvard University Press, 1970, pp. 221-238.

Thompson, E.P. *The Making of the English Working Class.* London: Gollancz, 1963.

Tilly, Charles, and James Rule. *Measuring Political Upheaval.* Princeton: Princeton University Press, 1965.

Notes

Introduction

1. The book that typifies this approach is Edouard Dolléans, *Histoire du mouvement ouvrier,* 3 vols. (Paris, 1936–1953).
2. The techniques of historical demography are described in Michel Fleury and Louis Henry, *Des registres paroissiaux à l'histoire de la population: manuel de dépouillement et d'exploitation de l'état civil ancien* (Paris, 1956), and *Nouveau Manuel de dépouillement et d'exploitation de l'état civil ancien* (Paris, 1965); E.A. Wrigley, ed., *An Introduction to English Historical Demography* (London, 1966). See also *Annales du demographie historique,* 1964–, *passim.*
3. Remi Gossez, *Les Ouvriers de Paris,* Société d'Histoire de la Révolution de 1848, vol. XXIV (Paris, 1967), 203.
4. Michelle Perrot, "Grèves, grévistes et conjoncture. Vieux problème, travaux neufs," *Le Mouvement Social,* no. 63 (1968), 115.
5. See Robert S. and Helen M. Lynd, *Middletown: A Study in Contemporary American Culture* (New York: Harcourt Brace & Co., 1929) which treats the experience of glassworkers in Muncie, Indiana, in these terms.
6. The work of Dolléans, *Histoire du mouvement ouvrier* here again is typical. See also articles in *Le Mouvement Social, passim.*

Chapter 1. Carmaux, 1850-1890

1. Robert Forster, *The Nobility of Toulouse in the Eighteenth Century* (Baltimore, 1960): see also Harvey Goldberg, *The Life of Jean Jaurès* (Madison, Wis., 1962), 97-98.

2. André Armengaud, *Les Populations de l'Est-Aquitain au début de l'époque contemporaine* (Paris, 1961), 260.

3. Jean Vareilles, "Carmaux (18 brumaire 1799 au 2 décembre 1851)," *Revue du Tarn*, no. 47 (1967), 344.

4. Ibid., 329-348.

5. A.D. Tarn, IV M 7 197.

6. Ibid.

7. Harvey Goldberg, *Jean Jaurès*, 97-98; Rolande Trempé, *Les Mineurs de Carmaux, 1848-1914* (Paris, 1971), 37-52.

8. Armengaud, *Les Populations de l'Est-Aquitain*, 260.

9. Trempé, *Les Mineurs de Carmaux*, 293.

10. A.M. Carmaux, Liste nominative de dénombrement de population, 1866 and 1876.

11. Henri Viguier, *Evolution démographique dans le département du Tarn depuis le début du XIXe siècle* (Albi, 1950), 27-29; A.D. Tarn, VI M 2 20 (Dénombrement de population, Commune de Carmaux, 1891).

12. Trempé, *Les Mineurs de Carmaux*, 292-293.

13. A.D. Tarn, IV M 7 197.

14. Trempé, *Les Mineurs de Carmaux*, 285.

Chapter 2. The Craft of the Glassworker

1. This definition is based in part on E.J. Hobsbawm's description of a labor aristocracy; see "The Labour Aristocracy in Nineteenth Century Britain," in *Labouring Men: Studies in the History of Labour* (New York, 1964), 321-370.

2. France, Direction du Travail, *Les Associations professionnelles ouvrières*, 4 vols. (Paris, 1899-1904), III, 591.

3. A.M. Carmaux, Registre de la paroisse de Cramaux (sic), 1712-1789.

4. A.D. Tarn, A.S., Carton 7, Côte 220.

5. Léon de Seilhac, *Une Enquête sociale: La grève de Carmaux et la verrerie d'Albi* (Paris, 1897), 6.

6. Ibid., 8; Trempé, *Les Mineurs de Carmaux*, 51.

7. A.D. Tarn, A.S., Cartons 12, 16, 61, and 62.

8. Diderot, D'Alembert, et al., *Encyclopédie ou Dictionnaire Raisonné des Sciences, des Arts et des Métiers,* vol. 17 (Paris, 1771), 94.

9. Ibid., 94–95.

10. Ibid., 95.

11. Ibid., 96.

12. See François-Georges Dreyfus, "L'Industrie de la verrerie en Bas-Languedoc de Colbert à la revolution industrielle du XIXe siècle," *Annales du Midi,* 63 (1951), 43–70; Warren C. Scoville, *Capitalism and French Glassmaking, 1640–1789* (Berkeley, 1950), 70–87; Saint-Quirnin, *Les Verriers de Languedoc, 1290–1790,* Extrait du bulletin de la société languedocienne de géographie, XXVII–XXIX (Montpellier, 1904–1906), 80; A. Sauzay, *La Verrerie, dupuis les temps les plus reculés jusqu'à nos jours* (Paris, 1868).

13. Scoville, *Capitalism and French Glassmaking,* 71; A.D. Tarn, A.S., Carton 16; Seilhac, *Une Enquête sociale,* 6–8.

14. A.D. Tarn, A.S., Carton 12.

15. Saint-Quirnin, *Les Verriers de Languedoc,* 194–195; Forster adds that "new glass factories built at Toulouse in 1786 and 1789 were operated by bourgeois owners," *Nobility of Toulouse,* 98.

16. *Les Associations professionnelles ouvrières,* III, 598.

17. A.M. Carmaux, Registre de la paroisse de Cramaux (sic) 1712–1789.

18. A.D. Tarn, A.S., Cartons 12 and 16.

19. A.M. Carmaux, Actes de Mariages.

20. A.D. Tarn, XIII M 6 17.

21. A.D. Tarn, A.S., Carton 12.

22. "This income advantage of glassworkers should not appear wholly surprising since they were of noble lineage and probably more highly skilled than ordinary artisans." Scoville, *Capitalism and French Glassmaking,* 75.

23. Statistique Générale, *Statistique annuelle,* 1871, 220.

24. Statistique Générale, *Statistique annuelle* (nouvelle série, XII), 1882.

25. A.D. Tarn, IV M 2 68.

26. *Troisième Congrès des verriers, premier congrès international tenu à Fourmies du 14 au 18 juillet 1892* (Lyon, 1892).

27. Seilhac, *Une Enquête sociale,* 52.

28. Report of Louis Renoux to the Paris Exposition of 1900. (I

used a handwritten copy in Renoux's private archives, kindly lent to me by his son.)

29. In the early twentieth century the contrast was even more striking, while the average age of death of miners was 54 years, 4 months in 1903–1912, it was 35 years, 6 months for glassworkers, Trempé, *Les Mineurs de Carmaux*, 316.

30. Ibid., 316.

31. It was almost impossible to devise an accurate measure of family size for glassworkers. High rates of population turnover made the determinations of completed family size impossible and the relatively small numbers of glassworkers in Carmaux's population make dubious the accuracy of age-specific fertility calculations. Crude measures of average household size, reached by averaging the number of children per family in a census listing, show that the average number of children per family was between 1.5 and 2 during 1866–1876. Trempé says that miners in this period had a "coefficient of fecundity" of 4. *Les Mineurs de Carmaux*, 314.

32. A.M. Carmaux, Registre de la paroisse de Cramaux (sic).

33. Vareilles, "Carmaux pendant la Grande Révolution Française," *Revue du Tarn*, no. 41 (1966), 70.

34. Scoville, *Capitalism and French Glassmaking*, 81.

35. A.D. Tarn, A.S., Carton 61.

36. A.D. Tarn, A.S., Cartons 12 and 16.

37. Ibid.

38. These calculations, based on family reconstitution, are more reliable than those based only on censuses. More sources of information are used, thus permitting a more careful determination of which glassworkers left and which stayed. Departures attributable to death can be determined as well.

Although more difficult to trace, since data were collected about glassworkers rather than specific individuals, changes in occupation were possible to follow: In this period, glassworkers rarely disappeared from our lists because they changed jobs; either they died or left Carmaux.

39. A.M. Carmaux, Liste nominative de population: 1876, 1881, 1886, 1891; Actes de Mariages: 1879, 1881, 1904, 1905, 1909, 1910, 1911; Actes de Naissances: 1881, 1882, 1884, 1886, 1888, 1890, 1892, 1900, 1905, 1907; Actes de Décès: 1882, 1883, 1894, 1899, 1908, 1909.

40. A.M. Carmaux, Liste nominative de population, 1876.

41. A.M. Carmaux, Liste nominatives de population, 1866, 1886, 1896; Actes de Mariages: 1867, 1910, 1911; Actes de Naissances: 1870, 1875, 1879, 1885, 1887, 1896, 1898, 1903, 1905, 1906, 1910, 1911; Acte de Décès: 1896. Also A.D. Tarn, IV M 2 95.

42. *Le Reveil des Verriers,* 15 janvier 1893.

43. During an interview with Mme Gaubat, on January 8, 1969, she referred frequently to the difficulties her family had in speaking to miners and peasants in Carmaux. Mme Gaubat is the daughter of a glassworker who arrived in Carmaux in 1884. In speaking of glassworkers in the town, Mme Gaubat recalled that they were "always badly adjusted to Carmaux. They did not speak the *patois*; they lived together near the Verrerie. It was difficult for them to adjust to life in Carmaux . . . [and] to form relationships with the miners."

Chapter 3. Glassworkers and Miners: A Contrast

1. A.D. Tarn, IV M 2 68.

2. Records consulted include: A.N. BB 18, BB 30, F 7, and F 12; A.D. Tarn, series M and U; local and national newspapers (see bibliography).

3. A.N. BB 18 dossiers 1450, 1525, 1530; A.N. F 12 4656; Statistique générale, *Statistique annuelle, 1882,* 135; *Les Associations professionnelles ouvrières,* III, 587–670; J.-P. Aguet, *Les Grèves sous la Monarchie de Juillet, 1830–1847* (Geneva, 1954), 30, 353, 401; Jean Maitron, *Dictionnaire biographique du mouvement ouvrier français* (Paris, 1964), II, 283; Octave Festy, *Le Mouvement ouvrier au début de la Monarchie de Juillet, 1830–1834* (Paris, 1908), 133.

4. A.D. Tarn, X M 3 3; Trempé, *Les Mineurs de Carmaux,* 69–71, 147.

5. See *Les Associations professionnelles ouvrières,* III, 587–670; Pierre Pelletier, *Les Verriers dans le Lyonnais et le Forez* (Paris, 1887); A. Charneau, *Note sur les fours et appareils de verreries* (Paris, 1886); Pierre Piganiol, *Le Verre, son histoire, sa technique* (Paris, 1965).

6. Trempé, *Les Mineurs de Carmaux,* 37–52. (The company became a Société Anonyme in 1861.)

7. Ibid., 199.

8. Ibid., 211, 212, 214, 249–50, 334.

221

9. Ibid., 262. This created and coincided with a housing shortage in Carmaux which gave miners little choice but to live in the *cité ouvrière.*

10. Ibid., 511-512.

11. A.N. BB 18 1525, 1530; Festy, *Le Mouvement ouvrier,* 132–133. (The strike at Rive-de-Gier in 1832 seems to have involved wages, but only indirectly. Apparently glassworkers there traditionally accepted lowered wages only after examining their employers' books. In 1832, enforcement of this tradition seems to have been at stake.)

12. Trempé, *Les Mineurs de Carmaux,* 182.

13. Ibid., 183.

14. Armengaud, *Les Populations de L'Est-Aquitain,* 260.

15. Trempé, *Les Mineurs de Carmaux,* 172.

16. A.D. Tarn, IV M 2 68.

17. Trempé, *Les Mineurs de Carmaux,* 360.

18. A.D. Tarn, IV M 2 68.

19. A.D. Tarn, IV M 2 64; also cited in Trempé, *Les Mineurs de Carmaux,* 528.

20. Trempé, *Les Mineurs de Carmaux,* 529–531.

21. Ibid., 115, 512.

22. Ibid., 201.

23. Ibid., 204–205.

24. A.D. Tarn, IV M 2 64.

25. Trempé, *Les Mineurs de Carmaux,* 124, 544, respectively.

26. Ibid., 546, and A.D. Tarn, IV M 2 64.

27. Trempé, *Les Mineurs de Carmaux,* 692–693.

28. Ibid., 738.

29. A.N. F 1 C III Tarn 12.

30. Trempé, *Les Mineurs de Carmaux,* 738.

31. *Les Associations professionnelles ouvrières,* III, 599–600.

32. Ibid., 620.

33. Ibid., 599, 622, and A.N. BB 18 1530.

34. Trempé, *Les Mineurs de Carmaux,* 162, 281.

35. Ibid., 187.

36. Jean-Baptiste Calvignac, "Mémoires d'un militant mineur: J.-B. Calvignac, maire de Carmaux," présentés par Rolande Trempé, *Le Mouvement Social,* no. 43 (1963), 121–138.

37. Stephan Thernstrom, "Working Class Social Mobility in

Industrial America," in Melvin Richter, ed., *Essays in Theory and History* (Cambridge, Mass., 1970), 225.

38. A.M. Carmaux, Matrices cadastrale.

39. There are a very few references, with little information, to glassworkers forming associations during the early nineteenth century. Festy says an association existed among the glassworkers of Rive-de-Gier in 1832. See his *Le Mouvement ouvrier*, 132–33. There were also appeals for funds made by two glassworker producers' cooperatives to the Conseil d'Encouragement pour les associations ouvrières in 1848. One of the associations seems to have been led by men who were quite old and who sought a certain secruity in their old age, but there is too little evidence to determine anything about the organization, purpose, and leadership of these associations. See Octave Festy, ed., *Procès verbaux du Conseil d'Encouragement pour les associations ouvrières, 11 juillet 1848–24 octobre 1849* (Paris, 1917), 103–105, 149, 168–170, 179.

Chapter 4. Mechanization

1. M.S. 4721, "Verrerie de Carmaux—Préliminaires," Rapport par E. de Planet, 30 novembre 1883.

2. Edouard Didron et Clémandot, *Rapport sur les cristaux, la verrerie, et les vitraux*, Exposition Universelle Internationale de 1878 à Paris (Paris, 1880), 23, 40.

3. Ibid., 22.

4. Goldberg, *Jean Jaurès*, 138.

5. Seilhac, *Une Enquête sociale*, 6–25. See also A. Masselin, "Causerie scientifique: Le verre," *Le Reveil des Verriers*, 8 juillet 1894; "Le Progrès," *Le Reveil des Verriers*, 1 janvier 1893; Gilbert Grandjean, "L'Avenir de la corporation," *Le Reveil des Verriers*, 9 septembre 1893; and Piganiol, *Le Verre*, 93–101; 196–218.

6. Didron et Clémandot, *Rapport*, 40.

7. A.D. Tarn, X M 3 3.

8. A.M. Carmaux, Liste nominative de population, 1876, 1881, 1886, 1891.

9. The molds were made of wood, brick, cast iron, or bronze, depending on the type of glass desired and the use to which the bottle would be put. Champagnes required different glass from

ordinary wines, carbonated liquids needed different glass from mineral water.

10. Masselin, "Causerie scientifique."
11. Seilhac, *Une Enquête sociale,* 8.
12. A.D. Tarn, *Statuts de la chambre syndicale des verriers de Carmaux,* 1892.
13. "Procès verbaux du 4ᵉ congrès national des travailleurs du verre, tenu à Bordeaux du 13 à 17 juillet, 1893," *Le Reveil des Verriers,* 4 mars et 11 mars 1894.
14. "Since the transformation of *fours à pots* into *fours à gaz* our wages have declined because individual production has increased enormously; the glass industry has been messed up by apprentices in a most terrible way; the number of grands garçons and souffleurs has sky-rocketed, creating an overabundance of workers . . . and, therefore, unemployment. Haven't we seen, *o scandale,* fifteen year old souffleurs and grands garçons of twelve?" "A Megecoste, par le syndicat," *Le Reveil des Verriers,* 12 novembre 1893.
15. "Réflexions d'un groupe de verriers," *Le Reveil des Verriers,* 19 novembre 1893.
16. Trempé, *Les Mineurs de Carmaux,* 183.
17. *Annuaire Statistique de la France,* 1889, 1895.
18. Statistique générale de la France. *Annuaire Statistique,* 1882, and 1891–1893.
19. Michelle Perrot emphasizes the importance to workers of decreases in nominal wages in "Grèves, grévistes et conjoncture," 121–122.
20. Didron et Clémandot, *Rapport,* 24.
21. A.D. Tarn, IV M 2 74.
22. Michel Vernay, "La Question d'apprentissage," *Le Reveil des Verriers,* 15 janvier 1893.
23. High rates of unemployment do not account for the high rates of turnover and the lack of correlation between numbers employed at the Verrerie Sainte Clothilde and numbers arriving and departing Carmaux in the 1870's. Rates of unemployment for French glassworkers rose only after the introduction of fours à gaz and moules fermés, in the 1880's.
24. A.M. Carmaux, Liste nominative de population, 1876, 1881, 1886, 1891; Actes de Mariages, 1879, 1881, 1904, 1905, 1909, 1910, 1911; Actes de Naissances, 1881, 1882, 1884, 1888, 1890, 1891, 1892, 1894, 1895, 1897, 1900, 1908, 1912; Actes de Décès, 1882, 1883, 1894, 1899, 1908, 1909.

25. A.M. Carmaux, Liste nominative de population, 1881, 1886, 1891, 1896; Actes de Mariages, 1889, 1902, 1907; Actes de Naissances, 1887, 1890, 1892, 1895, 1902, 1903, 1908, 1912; Actes de Décès, 1891, 1894, 1908.

26. Trempé, *Les Mineurs de Carmaux*, 315–316. The data on glassworkers was drawn from A.M. Carmaux, Actes de Décès.

27. A.D. Tarn, XII M 11 27, *Statuts de la Chambre syndicale des verriers de Carmaux*, 1891. A separate organization of auxiliary personnel was formed in 1892. The Chambre syndicale des ouvriers forgerons, frappeurs, gaziers, dégrilleurs, composeurs, ajusteurs, et similaires de la verrerie de Carmaux had only 80 members at its beginning. The number of auxiliaries ever unionized was always small, and their union always followed the lead of the glassworkers. See A.D. Tarn, XIII M 11 4.

28. *Fédération des verriers de France. Deuxième congrès tenu à Lyon du 1er au 6 septembre 1891* (Lyon, 1892).

29. A. Gibon, *La Grève de Carmaux* (Paris, 1893); Goldberg, *Jean Jaurès*, 138; Seilhac, *Une Enquête sociale*, 32, 60–75.

30. Claude Willard, *Le Mouvement socialiste en France (1893–1905): Les Guesdistes* (Paris, 1965), 50, 63.

31. Seilhac, *Une Enquête sociale*, 108.

32. Fourteen glassworkers have been defined as leaders. A glassworker qualified as a leader for purposes of this study if he arrived in Carmaux before 1894. This year was used rather than 1895, the year of the strike, so that leadership had been exercised for more than one year. A glassworker qualified as a leader if he was referred to as such in more than one of the following categories of sources:
1. Police records: A.D. Tarn, IV M series
   A.N. BB 18 or BB 30; F 7
   A.D. Tarn, Jugements Correctionnels
2. Union records: Minutes of the local union, 1894
   Congresses of the National Federation of Glassworkers
   Le Reveil des Verriers; as author of union brochures or pamphlets
3. Political records: Listed as socialist candidate for municipal office
   Noted in *La Voix des Travailleurs*
4. Historical and oral accounts: Secondary works, books, and articles
   Interviews with former glassworkers or their children

33. Renoux and Gidel were married on the same day. See A.M. Carmaux, Acte de Mariage, 22 décembre 1894.

34. A.M. Carmaux, Acte de Mariage, 11 novembre 1890.

35. *Le Reveil des Verriers*, 12 août 1894. For some historians of French socialism, see Dolléans, *Le Mouvement ouvrier*; Goldberg, *Jean Jaurès*; Trempé, *Les Mineurs de Carmaux*. Willard, *Les Guesdistes*.

36. *Le Reveil des Verriers*, 29 octobre 1893.

37. *Fédération des verriers de France. Deuxième congrès tenu à Lyon du 1er au 6 septembre 1891*, 68.

38. *Fédération nationale des travailleurs du verre. Congrès national tenu à Marseille, du 21 au 27 juillet 1895* (Lyon, 1895), 52.

39. *Troisième congrès des verriers tenu à Fourmies du 14 au 18 juillet 1892* (Lyon, 1892), 65.

40. The average age of the glassworkers arriving in Carmaux was difficult to determine. The closest approximation can be derived from the graphs of age based on the censuses. (See Fig. 2.)

41. A.M. Carmaux, Liste nominative de population, 1866, 1872, 1876; Acte de Décès, 1894; "Funérailles du citoyen Camille Pradel," *Le Reveil des Verriers*, 4 novembre 1894.

42. A.D. Tarn, IV M 2 75, IV M 2 85.

43. Willard, *Les Guesdistes*, 50, 63; Calvignac once described Charpentier and Aucouturier, "who came from Montluçon," as "enfiefed to a party to which I did not belong." "Mémoires d'un militant mineur: J.-B. Calvignac, maire de Carmaux," 137.

44. A.M. Carmaux, Liste nominative de population, 1891; Acte de Mariage, 1894.

45. "Vaincre ou Mourir—à la mémoire de Philippe Renoux," *Le Reveil des Verriers*, 21 janvier 1894.

46. *Le Reveil des Verriers*, 29 octobre 1893.

47. *Status de la Chambre syndicale des verriers de Carmaux;* A.D. Tarn, XIII M 11 27.

48. A.R., Minutes of the Chambre syndicale des verriers de Carmaux, Rapport du conseil syndical du 8 julliet 1894.

49. A.R. Minutes, Réunion de Conseil syndical du 22 septembre 1894.

50. A.R., Minutes, Procès verbal du Conseil syndical du 6 mai 1894.

51. *Le Reveil des Verriers*, 1 mars 1893.

52. A.D. Tarn, IV M 2 74.

53. *Troisième congrès des verriers, premier congrès international tenu à Fourmies du 14 au 18 juillet 1892* (Lyon, 1892), 41.

54. "Le Dernier des métiers," *Le Reveil des Verriers,* 1 janvier 1893; Michel Vernay, "La Question de l'apprentissage devant notre prochain congrès de Bordeaux," *Le Reveil des Verriers,* 1 février 1893.

55. *Troisième congrès . . . à Fourmies . . . 1892,* 71.

56. *Deuxième congrès . . . à Lyon . . . 1891,* 58.

57. *Troisième congrès . . . à Fourmies . . . 1892,* 66.

58. Ibid., 51.

59. B. Tissot, "Evolution prolétarienne, principes sur lesquels nous devons nous baser pur l'avenir," *Le Reveil des Verriers,* 15 février 1893.

60. *Deuxième congrès . . . à Lyon . . . 1891,* 67-68.

61. *Le Reveil des Verriers,* 1 mars 1893; 15 juin 1893.

62. *Cinquième congrès . . . à Marseille . . . 1895,* 52.

Chapter 5. Socialism

1. A.D. Tarn, IV M 2 68.

2. See Trempé, *Les Mineurs de Carmaux,* 899, on the variety of political loyalties of Carmaux's miners.

3. Bernard H. Moss, "Origins of the French Labor Movement: The Socialism of Skilled Workers," unpub. diss., Columbia University, 1972, 12.

4. *La Voix des Travailleurs,* 12 mai 1889.

5. Trempé, *Les Mineurs de Carmaux,* 558-559.

6. Ibid.

7. Ibid., 513-516.

8. Ibid., 536.

9. Ibid., 759.

10. *Le Reveil des Verriers,* 1 janvier 1893.

11. Trempé, *Les Mineurs de Carmaux,* 816.

12. Ibid., 793.

13. Ibid., 794.

14. *La Voix des Travailleurs,* 1 mai 1891.

15. Direction du Travail, *Statistique des grevès et des recours à la conciliation 1890–1892* (published as no. 3 of *Notices et comptes rendus* (Paris, 1892), 112.

16. The growing numbers of such clubs can be followed in *La Voix des Travailleurs,* 1891–1895, *passim.*

17. Goldberg, *Jean Jaurès,* 105–106; and Willard, *Les Guesdistes,* 68.

18. Goldberg, *Jean Jaurès*, 60–61.
19. Ibid., 60.
20. Ibid., 100.
21. In a sense the unions fulfilled the role envisioned for them by Fernand Pelloutier, the theorist of revolutionary syndicalism. Pelloutier defined the *bourses du travail* as centers of working-class culture. He saw them as a means of overturning the state and as the organizing institutions of a new society. His ideas must have been based, in part, on his observations of experiences like those of Carmaux's unions. See Alan Spitzer, "Anarchy and Culture: Fernand Pelloutier and the Dilemma of Revolutionary Syndicalism," *International Review of Social History*, 8 (1963), 379–388.
22. Trempé, *Les Mineurs de Carmaux*, 307.
23. A.D. Tarn, IV M 6 10.
24. *La Voix des Travailleurs*, 1 septembre 1892.
25. Ibid., 3 juillet 1892.
26. Ibid., 3 juillet 1892.
27. A.D. Tarn, IV M 6 10.
28. *La Voix des Travailleurs*, 26 avril 1891.
29. Ibid., 7 avril 1892.
30. Ibid., 26 avril 1891.
31. A.D. Tarn, IV M 2 72; A.N. BB 18 1887.
32. *La Voix des Travailleurs*, 3 septembre 1893, and 5 juin 1894, respectively.
33. Ibid., 7 février 1892.
34. Ibid., 3 juillet 1892.
35. Ibid., 14 octobre 1892.
36. *Le Reveil des Verriers*, 1 janvier 1893.
37. Ibid., 15 janvier 1893.
38. Ibid., 1 janvier 1893.
39. Ibid., 15 fevrier 1893.
40. *La Voix des Travailleurs*, 24 avril 1898; A.D. Tarn, IV M 2 85.
41. A.D. Tarn, IV M 2 76.
42. A.D. Tarn, IV M 2 75.
43. A.D. Tarn, IV M 6 10; see also "Mémoires d'un militant mineur: J.B. Calvignac, maire de Carmaux," 126.
44. Moss, "Origins of the French Labor Movement," 12–15, 23–24; Trempé attributes socialism in Carmaux to "outside influences." *Les Mineurs de Carmaux*, 864.
45. A.D. Tarn, IV M 2 85; *La Voix des Travailleurs*, 24 avril 1898; *Le Reveil des Verriers*, 1 and 15 janvier 1893.

46. A.D. Tarn, II M 7 197.
47. *La Voix des Travailleurs*, 17 mars 1889.
48. Ibid., 28 juillet 1889.
49. Ibid., 1 décembre 1889.
50. Ibid., 25 décembre 1892.
51. *Le Républicain de Carmaux*, 4 mai 1890.
52. *La Voix des Travailleurs*, 1 février 1891.
53. A.D. Tarn, T 1 C 2.
54. Despite a continuing improvement in real wages from 1883 to 1892, miners felt that the cost of living was rising, Trempé argues, because of expanded consumer needs. *Les Mineurs de Carmaux*, 412–413.
55. *La Voix des Travailleurs*, 22 mai 1892.
56. Ibid., 27 décembre 1891.
57. Ibid., 10 janvier 1892.
58. Willard, *Les Guesdistes*, 68, 70.
59. *La Voix des Travailleurs*, 8 mai 1892; Trempé, *Les Mineurs de Carmaux*, 892.
60. A.D. Tarn, II M 7 197.
61. *La Voix des Travailleurs*, 4 août 1892.
62. The account of the strike is based on Goldberg, *Jean Jaurès*, chap. v, and on Direction du Travail, *Notes et comptes rendus*, no. 3.
63. A.D. Tarn, Jugements correctionnels, no. 225, 29 octobre 1892; A.N. BB 18 dossier, 1887.
64. Direction du Travail *Notes et comptes rendus*, no. 3, 124.
65. A.N. BB 18, 1887.
66. A.D. Tarn, IV M 2 72
67. A.N. BB 18, 1887.
68. Goldberg, *Jean Jaurès*, 106.
69. Rolande Trempé, "L'Echec électoral de Jaurès à Carmaux, 1898," *Cahiers Internationaux*, no. 93 (1958), 47–64.
70. Ibid.
71. Goldberg, *Jean Jaurès*, 139; and A.D. Tarn, II M 7 197.
72. Direction du Travail, *Statistiques des grèves et des recours à la conciliation survenus pendant l'année 1895* (Paris, 1896), 253–255.
73. A.D. Tarn, IV M 2 74.

Chapter 6. The Strike of 1895

1. Two smaller strikes of *porteurs* in 1891 and of *similaires* in 1892 did not involve the skilled glassworkers and were quickly

settled in favor of the striking groups. A.D. Tarn, XIII M 6 9; *La Voix des Travailleurs*, 18 août 1892.

2. *Deuxième congrès . . . à Lyon . . . 1891.*

3. *Les Associations professionnelles ouvrières*, III, 647-648.

4. Ibid., 648.

5. "Aux Electeurs de Carmaux," *La Voix des Travailleurs*, 24 avril 1898; A. Galonnier, "Pour Marius Rauzier," *La Voix des Travailleurs*, 18 septembre 1898; J. Baudot, "Le Vieux Militant Rauzier," *La Voix des Travailleurs*, 1, 9, et 23 octobre 1898.

6. *Le Reveil des Verriers*, 12 octobre 1894.

7. A.R., Minutes de la Chambre syndicale des verriers de Carmaux, *passim*.

8. *La Voix des Travailleurs*, 25 avril 1895.

9. *Statistiques des grèves*, 1895, 244-266, *passim*.

10. Seilhac, *Une Enquête sociale*, 74; *Statistiques des grèves*, 1895, 247-248.

11. M.S., Carton 5.655-6.

12. *La Voix des Travailleurs*, 25 avril 1895.

13. *Statistiques des grèves*, 1895, 254.

14. Ibid., 253.

15. Ibid., 253.

16. Ibid., 248.

17. Ibid., 264.

18. Ibid., 250.

19. Ibid., 251.

20. Ibid., 251.

21. Ibid., 247; A.D. Tarn, XIII M 9 6; A.N. BB 18, 2010; Jean Jaurès, *La Grève de Carmaux* (1895), 41. (This brochure was a reprint of Jaurès' speeches to the Chamber of Deputies on October 24 and 25, 1896.)

22. *Statistiques des grèves, 1895*, 255; Jaurès, *La Grève de Carmaux*, 42.

23. Jaurès, *La Grève de Carmaux*, 41.

24. A.D. Tarn, *Jugements correctionnels*, no. 314, 5 octobre 1895; A.N. BB 18, 2010.

25. A.N. BB 18, 2010. *La Voix des Travailleurs*, 3 octobre 1895.

26. A.N. BB 18, 2010.

27. *Statistiques des grèves, 1895*, 255.

28. *Le Temps*, 6 novembre 1895.

29. M.S., Carton 5.655-6.

30. A.N. BB 18, 2010; A.D. Tarn, *Jugements correctionnels*, nos. 310 and 315.
31. Jaurès, *La Grève de Carmaux*, 36.
32. Quoted in Goldberg, *Jean Jaurès*, 143.
33. *Statistiques des grèves*, 1895, 264.
34. Ibid., 264.
35. Ibid., 265.
36. *La Voix des Travailleurs*, 1 décembre 1895 and 7 janvier 1896.
37. *La Dépêche de Toulouse*, 7 janvier 1896, cited in Léon de Seilhac, *La Verrerie Ouvrière d'Albi* (Paris, 1903), 39.
38. *La Voix des Travailleurs*, 16 janvier 1896.
39. Rolande Trempé, "Jaurès et la Verrerie Ouvrière," in Trempé, ed. *Actes du Colloque Jaurès et la Nation*, (Toulouse, 1965), 13.
40. Marien Baudot, "La Chambre syndicale des Verriers de Carmaux," *La Voix des Travailleurs*, 16 janvier 1896.
41. *La Voix des Travailleurs*, 16 janvier 1896.
42. Trempé, "Jaurès et la Verrerie Ouvrière," 15.
43. Trempé, *Les Mineurs de Carmaux*, 892.
44. Ibid., 762.
45. Ibid., 756, 762.
46. *Les Associations professionnelles ouvrières*, III, 518–519.
47. Trempé, *Les Mineurs de Carmaux*, 777. It remains to be seen if the *crise syndicale* in these years was (1) peculiar to Carmaux, (2) peculiar to specific trades, or (3) a national phenomenon. It clearly does not seem to be a national phenomenon since certain trades experienced steady increases in union membership from 1890 to 1900. The metal and building trades and transport workers unions showed no signs of crisis in the 90's. On the other hand *ameublement* and *cuirs et peaux* seem to have had experiences similar to the glass-workers. It may well have been that 1895 marked a turning point for some artisan trades like glassworkers. Work remains to be done on this question, as well as on the question of the miners—a group not really comparable to other artisanal trades. Trempé finds union developments similar to Carmaux's in the Nord and in the Pas-de-Calais, but says they were caused by different local factors (*Les Mineurs de Carmaux*, 1049). Furthermore, the categories of trades used in *Les Associations professionnelles ouvrières* must be broken down into separate occupational groups so they may be more thoroughly examined. See *Les Associations professionnelles ouvrières*, vols. I–IV.

Chapter 7. New Glassworkers and Old, 1896–1914

1. Rolande Trempé, "Jaurès et la Verrerie Ouvrière," in *Actes du Colloque Jaurès et la nation*, edited by l'Association des publications de la Faculté des Lettres et Sciences humains de Toulouse (Toulouse, 1965), 1.
2. *La Voix des Travailleurs*, 1 décembre 1895.
3. Ibid., 7 janvier 1896.
4. Ibid., 19 décembre 1895.
5. This finding questions, if it does not refute, the assumptions that most artisans move into factories when their trades are mechanized. In the case of French glassworkers, the idea of a one-to-one relationship between the "proletarianization" of artisans and the industrialization of their trades does not work. An example of this assumption is in Robert M. and Helen Lynd, *Middletown: A Study in Contemporary American Culture*, (New York, 1929).
6. *La Voix des Travailleurs*, 28 avril 1896.
7. A.D. Tarn, IV M 2 95.
8. A.D. Tarn, IV M 2 95.
9. A.D. Tarn, IV M 2 95.
10. Seilhac, *La Verrerie Ouvrière d'Albi*, 157–159.
11. Maurice Talmeyr, "Chez les verriers," *Revue des Deux Mondes* (1 février 1898), 661–662.
12. A.D. Tarn, IV M 2 97.
13. E. Geugnot and E. Guérard, *La Verité sur la Verrerie Ouvrière; sa création, ses résultats, par des ouvriers renvoyés* (Albi, 1897), 92.
14. A.D. Tarn, IV M 2 97.
15. "Règlements de la Verrerie Ouvrière," in Seilhac, *La Verrerie Ouvrière*, 118-121; and Talmeyr, "Chez les verriers," 656.
16. See Chap. 2 and Table 8 above.
17. Trempé, *Les Mineurs de Carmaux*, 337; A.D. Tarn, IV M 2 95.
18. Trempé, *Les Mineurs de Carmaux*, 337.
19. Ibid., 148.
20. Ibid., 158.
21. Ibid., 777.
22. *Le Cri des Travailleurs*, 7 mai 1899.
23. A.D. Tarn, IV M 4 25 (Rapport no. 2978/1048: 5e Congrès de la Fédération Nationale des Verriers, Albi, 1906).
24. A.D. Tarn, IV M 2 95.
25. Ibid.
26. Ibid.

27. Ibid.
28. Ibid.
29. Ibid.
30. A.D. Tarn, IV M 2 64.
31. A.D. Tarn, XIII M 11 27. (Statuts de la chambre syndicale des verriers de Carmaux, 15 février 1900.)
32. A.D. Tarn, IV M 4 25.
33. A.D. Tarn, XIII M 11 27.
34. A.D. Tarn, IV M 2 95.
35. Seilhac, *La Verrerie Ouvrière*, 118–120.
36. Ibid., 100–101; A.D. Tarn, IV M 2 97; and *Conservation des Hypothèques d'Albi*, vol. 873, no. 36.
37. A.R., Minutes of the Chambre syndicale des verriers de Carmaux, 1894, *passim*.
38. *Statistiques des grèves*, 1895, 247–248.
39. Pelletier, *Les Verriers dans le Lyonnais*, 210–212.
40. Ibid., and A.D. Tarn, A.S., A.M. Carmaux, Actes Civiles, *passim*.
41. Talmeyr, "Chez les verriers," 652–653; A.D. Tarn, IV M 2 95; A.R., "Verrerie Ouvrière: inscrits sur le registre du paie, année, 1896."
42. A.D. Tarn, IV M 2 97.
43. A.D. Tarn, IV M 2 95, and IV M 2 97.
44. A.D. Tarn, IV M 2 97.
45. Geugnot and Guérard, *La Verité sur La Verrerie Ouvrière*.
46. Ibid., 80–81.
47. Ibid., 23.
48. Seilhac, *La Verrerie Ouvrière*, 126–127.
49. *Fédération Française des Travailleurs du Verre, Congrès national* (28 septembre–1 octobre 1903), 45.
50. Ibid., 52.
51. *Fédération Française des Travailleurs du Verre, Congrès national* (1903), 57.
52. *Les Associations professionnelles ouvrières*, III, 670.
53. Ibid.
54. Ibid., 668; and *Le Reveil des Verriers*, 13 décembre 1896.
55. *Fédération Nationale des Travailleurs du Verre, Congrès national* (Paris, le 15–16 septembre 1902).
56. *Fédération Française des Travailleurs du Verre, Congrès national* (1903), 60–61.
57. Ibid.

58. A.D. Tarn, IV M 4 25.

59. *Congrès national* (1903), 60–61.

60. The tone and outlook of the glassworkers' national Federation of 1902 changed as the Boucher machine became the predominant means of producing bottles. By the 1920's, the glassworkers union was an industrial union whose members were unskilled or semi-skilled workers. The concerns and activities of this union, though again militant, were different from those of the 1890's and early 1900's. The new phase of trade-union militance needs further study. It is, however, beyond the concern and scope of this book.

61. We have no direct data to confirm this statement. The indirect evidence, however, seems overwhelming: (1) the children of leaders all followed this pattern and (2) glassworker children in Carmaux and Albi entered neither glass factories nor the mines. There are repeated individual cases of them becoming white-collar workers. Geographic mobility and the sheer number of individuals moving to different places made further precision impossible.

Epilogue. Three Portraits

1. A.D. Tarn, A.S. carton 12.
2. Ibid.
3. Scoville, *Capitalism and French Glassmaking,* 71.
4. A.D. Tarn, A.S., carton 12.
5. A.M. Blaye, Liste nominative de population, 1861.
6. Ibid.
7. A.M. Carmaux, Acte de Mariage, 12 juin 1890.
8. A.D. Tarn, II M 7 197.
9. A.M. Carmaux, Liste nominatives des population, 1886, 1891, 1896.
10. A.R., Minutes, Rapport du Conseil syndical, 28 juin 1894.
11. A.N., BB 18, 2010.
12. A.D. Tarn, IV M 2 83.
13. Ibid.
14. A.M. Carmaux, Liste nominative de population. . . . 1891.
15. A.D. Tarn, IV M 2 85, IV M 2 75.
16. A.M. Carmaux, Acte de Mariage, 20 mars 1890.
17. A.D. Tarn, IV M 2 85.
18. Calvignac, "Mémoires d'un militant mineur: J.-B. Calvignac, maire de Carmaux," 137.

19. A.D. Tarn, IV M 2 85.
20. A.D. Tarn, IV M 2 97.
21. A.M. Carmaux, Acte de Naissance, 5 mars 1896.
22. Liste nominative des porteurs . . . 1895 (in a collection of papers lent me by Rolande Trempé).
23. A.M. Carmaux, Actes de Mariages, 1906, 1907.

Index

Alary, Jean-Baptiste, 193-197
Albar, Emile Augustin, 199-200
Albi, population of, 9
Anticlericalism, 119-122, 128
Apprenticeship, *See* Glassworkers,
apprenticeship
Aucouturier, Michel, 87, 89, 115,
120, 123, 155, 178, 182, 183, 184,
196-199; elected to Municipal
Council, 198
Auriol, Jules Vincent, 199

Baudot, Jean (Marien), 87, 89, 90,
96, 97, 142, 161, 177, 178, 182,
183, 184; elected to Conseil
d'Arrondissement, 137, 146; in
strike of *1895*, 143-145
Boucher machine, 170, 177; effects
at Verrerie Sainte Clothilde, 178,
187
Bouteillé, Hippolyte, 126

Calvignac, Jean-Baptiste, 69, 121,
132, 134, 160, 198; elected to
Conseil d'Arrondissement, 132,
136-137, Mayor of Carmaux, 109,
131, 136-137
Carmaux: canton of, 14, 126; infant
mortality rates, 43; Municipal

Council, 11, 17, 46, 115, 125;
population density, 17; population
growth, 7, 12, 16, 17, 18; social
structure, 9-11, 16
Cassier, Jean, 49
Castres, population of, 9
Cercle des Travailleurs, 118, 120,
124, 125
Chambre syndicale des ouvriers
verriers et similaires d'Albi, 184
Chambre syndicale des verriers de
Carmaux, 87, 92, 107, 113-114,
123, 198; organization of, 98-99;
statutes, 98, 179
Charpentier, Maximilien, 88, 89, 91,
106, 141, 155, 156, 182, 183
Chaubard, Jean-Louis, 50
Civil baptism, 122
Civil burials, 120, 121
Civil marriages, 120
Claussé, Philippe, 90, 105, 150
Confédération Générale du Travail,
177, 188

Demographic records, uses of, 2, 35

Elections: *1889*, 116, 125, 126;
1892, 14, 130, 131; *1893*, 135,
136; *1896*, 162, 196; *1898*, 162

Index

Fédération des Travailleurs du Tarn, 125, 126
Fédération du Verre, 87, 105, 123, 139, 140, 141, 145, 157, 188
Forster, Robert, 7
French glass manufacturers, 73
French labor movement: histories of, 1, 6; strikes, 4

Gamin, 19, 23, 31, 80. See also Glassworkers, apprenticeship
Gand, Nicolas, 86
Gand, Paul, 86
Gidel, Martin, 89, 121, 182, 183
Glass bottles, overproduction of, 74, 80, 81. See also Glassworkers
Glassworkers, 3, 4, 19, 23-34, 35, 36; ages, 23, 77, 80; apprenticeship, 19, 23, 31, 32-33, 79, 80, 94, 96, 98, 101-103, 104, 170; death rates, 43, 87; geographic mobility, 46-50, 68, 83-87, 91; geographic origins, 48, 79, 169, 170; health, 42, 43, 190; household size, 45; infant mortality, 43, 87; and miners contrasted, 42, 43, 54, 61, 108, 118, 119; occupational mobility, 34, 35, 36, 37, 100, 182-184, 190-191, 195; social origins, 34-35, 36, 79, 169, 170; social position, 20, 45; strikes, 54, 57, 67, 68, 91, 114, 139-142; union, 91-92, 152, 166, 177, 178; union leaders, 88, 92, 93, 94, 96, 108, 180, 181, 182, 183, 184, 225n; wages, 20, 34, 38-42, 60, 81, 82, 175
Gossez, Remi, 3
Grand Garçon, 23, 31, 80, 104. See also Glassworkers, apprenticeship
Griffuelhes, Victor, 177

Jaurès, Jean, 1, 109, 123, 127, 154, 155, 157, 160, 167, 198; election 1889, 116; election 1893, 135-136; election 1898, 162-163; glassworkers strike of 1895, 148, 149, 150; miners strike of 1892, 143

Mazamet, population of, 9
Mechanization, 3, 4, 188, 189, 191, 192. See also Boucher machine
Michon, Maximilien, 155
Minck, Paule, 124
Miners, 9, 10, 56, 57, 111, 112; ages of, 176; and glassworkers (see Glassworkers, and miners contrasted); death rates, 43; geographic origins, 69-70; grievances, 62-64, 65, 66, 112, 113; household size, 45; infant mortality, 43; occupational mobility, 63, 111-112; social origins, 58; social position, 17; strike of 1892, 114, 115, 133-136, 139 (see also Strikes, miners); strikes, 53, 54, 56, 60, 64 (see also Strikes, miners); union, 111, 164, 176; urban life style, 117; wages, 39, 59, 62-63
Moss, Bernard, 125
Municipal Council, see Carmaux, Municipal Council

National Federation of Glassworkers, 166, 177, 189, 199. See also Fédération du Verre

Parti Ouvrier Français, 109, 124, 130
Peguignot, Hippolyte, 49, 85
Peguignot, Jean-Claude, 49, 85
Pelloutier, Fernand, 109, 228n
Phylloxera, 81
Pradel, Camille, 93

Rauzier, Marius, 88, 121, 123, 124, 125, 127, 128, 141
Reille, Baron, 115-116
Rénard, Emile, 88, 93, 183
Renoux, Louis, 88, 89, 97, 182, 183, 184, 185, 186, 191
Renoux, Philippe, 88, 97
Rességuier, Fernand, 12, 17, 21, 73-74, 145, 146, 147, 149-151, 154, 157, 158, 159
Reveil des Verriers, Le, 100, 188
Revolution of 1848, 11

Salles, Auguste, 184
Scoville, Warren, 38, 46, 47
Siemens furnace, 73
Socialism, 5, 89, 110; defined in
  Carmaux, 109–110, 127; electoral
  strength in Carmaux, 163
Solages, Marquis de, 114, 115, 135;
  election of *1889*, 116; election of
  1898, 162
Solages château, 9, 10, 21
Solages family, social position, 10, 16
Souffleurs, 23, 32, 80, 104. *See also*
  Glassworkers
Strikes: glassworkers, 54, 57, 67, 68;
  strike of *1891*, 91, 114, 139–142;
  strike of *1895*, 1, 150–151, 158–
  159, 199; miners, 53, 54, 56, 60,
  64, 114, 133–136, 139
Syndicat des ouvriers mineurs de
  Carmaux, 112, 113, 114. *See also*
  Miners, union

Tarn, department of the, 7, 48, 79,
  169, 170; agricultural "crisis" in,
  58
Trempé, Rolande, 69, 117, 131, 164

Union, *See* Glassworkers, union;
  Miners, union

Verrerie Ouvrière d'Albi, 1, 160,
  168, 171, 172, 185, 186, 199;
  ownership, 182; regulations, 174,
  185; union at, 181; wages at, 171;
  workforce, 172, 174
Verrerie Royale, 9, 20, 21, 37, 38;
  contrasted with Verrerie Sainte
  Clothilde, 22, 23, 34
Verrerie Sainte Clothilde, 20–22, 39,
  80; workforce, 22, 54, 75; contrasted with Verrerie Royale, 22,
  23, 34. *See also* Verrerie Royale
Voix des Travailleurs, La, 125